"Reading this book opened my heart ⸺ ⸺ ⸺ What a beautiful and meaningful message. As a mental health therapist, who specializes in working with new mothers suffering with peripartum mood disorders, this book is exactly what new mothers need. Hearing stories of how Heavenly Father speaks to us and guides us even when the storms of mental health make it difficult to hear His voice. He is so very aware of mothers. We are not alone."

- Lail Berrett, CMHC

"Aubrey provides a safe space in this book. The connection and empathy you experience while reading is tangible. You connect with, and love women you have never even met before! He Came For Me re-emphasizes to the reader that she is not alone, no matter the circumstance, no matter the age. The real-life events may differ, but all of them turn you to the balm that only the Savior Jesus Christ can provide."

- Camille Laycock, ANYA Mentor

"He Came for Me will inspire you to see the Savior and His love, comfort and peace in your everyday life. I felt the admiration, respect, individual love, care and attention Heavenly Father has for motherhood and each of us. He is truly in the details, and will always come for us. I am thankful for Aubrey's vulnerability; for sharing her very personal moments that shaped her powerful testimony of Christ."

- Cheri Evans, Wellness Coach

"*He Came for Me* isn't just a book. It is a a collections of pages, truly brought to life by the experiences of -not only the author- but dozens of other woman; witnessing the power there is to be felt when we acknowledge the hand of a Father in Heaven who knows us personally and a Savior, Jesus Christ, who loves us more than we can comprehend. Every story shared made me feel closer to Heaven and even more affected by the touch of the Master's hand. There's a unique reverence and spirit in this book and I look forward to reading and sharing these stories again and again."

- Kelsee Boyer, Mental Health Advocate

"A beautiful and impactful book, penned with authenticity and candor, that will renew your hope, faith, and strength, as you witness the experiences of Christ coming to women. As you delve into its pages you will discover that He comes in the ugly, the mundane, the beautiful, and the heart-wrenching moments. He Came for Me, will leave you with a personal desire to intentionally look for ways that He has come to YOU, for YOU, and with YOU."

- Ariane Packer, Mental Health Advocate

"As I read each story of Christ coming to women, I quickly began to remember all the times my Savior has come for me throughout my life. Known and unknown. Seen and unseen. The teachings, inspiration, and spirit I felt from each page filled my eyes with tears and helped me feel just how much I am loved by my Savior, the Master Healer and Comforter. Though this was a collection of stories from different women, it felt personal as if they were my own and reminded me that as Christ comes to me daily, I too can go to Him- anytime, anywhere. I know this book will be a source of light for many individuals looking for Christ. You don't have to be a certain religion to be a reader of He Came For Me. This book will serve all those who want to feel Christ more, but also help people seek and expect miracles to happen in their lives because of Him."

- Sara Johnson, Life Coach

"These pages are filled with vulnerable, raw emotions and that can help you process and recognize your own experiences with the Savior. Aubrey's personal stories, coupled with the experiences of other striving women helps you know that you are not alone. There is an army of women surrounding you to support and understand you, as shown within these pages. Most importantly, we have a loving Savior who will be there with us in our darkest moments. It might be hard to recognize His hand or presence in the moment of deep despair, but through stillness, the light will come through the dark clouds. This book is a testimony of these moments, and I applaud the vulnerable hearts who shared some of their darkest moments to help me in mine."

- Cori Lazarte, Marriage + Family Therapist

He Came For Me

He Came For Me

Stories of Christ Coming to Modern-Day Women

Aubrey Grossen

Book design by Jenessa Kramer
All Images by Lori Adams
Edited by Maren Droubay

Visit us at www.aubreygrossen.com.
For mental health support: visit www.anewyouagain.com

Printed in the United States of America.

First Edition

ISBN 979-8-3961-9742-8 (Paperback)

Dedicated to my angel grandpa,
John Anderson, who lived a life for the
Savior and always advocated for women's
role in motherhood.

I'll always be a grandpa's girl.

Contents

Contents

Part 2: He Came For HER

Preface

"Perhaps it is no wonder that the women were first at the Cradle and last at the Cross. They had never known a man like this Man - there never has been such another."
Dorothy L. Sayers

During a work trip with my husband several years ago, I woke up one morning after he left, feeling inspired to share how Jesus Christ has come to me throughout my life.

I remember feeling completely overwhelmed with feelings about this message that needed to be shared. I spent a few hours processing my love for the Savior, and how I could adequately describe the different moments in which He has come for me.

In the scriptures you read of many accounts where Christ comes to women. The 'woman at the well' probably had a heavy heart and a lot on her to-do list, yet He was able to meet her at the well- right where she was- and offer the living water.

He came to Mary Magdalene after He was crucified and resurrected. Can you imagine the joy she felt in her heart when she saw Him, after thinking her best friend was gone forever? This experience emphasizes Jesus Christ's high regard for women, because Mary Magdalene was chosen as the first person to witness- and then be commissioned to testify of the resurrected Savior. The Lord continues to rely on women in our day to stand as witnesses of Him.

Elder M. Russell Ballard has declared, *"Our dispensation is not without its heroines. Countless women from every continent and walk of life have made dramatic contributions to the cause of Christ."*

Prophets climbed mountains to talk with God, and while there is beauty in that, I believe He comes to women- exactly where they are.

What I find even more fascinating, is that *Christ has never stopped coming* for women; in fact, the stories I've gathered for this book are proof that He *still* comes.

While we aren't meeting Him at a well or an empty tomb, He comes to us in tearful closets, quiet drives, hospital rooms, and kitchen floors (even- or should I say *especially*-sticky ones).

My hope is that you will read these modern-day accounts and witnesses of the Savior in the lives of women, and ponder on the times that He has come for you.

Part 1 :

He Came For Me : Aubrey's Story

"However late you think you are, however many chances you think you have missed, however many mistakes you feel you have made or talents you think you don't have, or however far from home and family and God you feel you have traveled, I testify that you have not traveled beyond the reach of divine love. It is not possible for you to sink lower than the infinite light of Christ's Atonement shines."
Jeffrey R. Holland

CHAPTER 1

He Came For Me On A Scooter

"I am encircled about eternally in the arms of his love."
2 Nephi 1:15

I could tell that she had a bad feeling. She hesitated, trying to figure out a stressful day where she literally wished she could be in two places at once.

"We can ride our scooters, Mom! We'll be safe! I promise!" my twelve-year-old self said, begging and looking up at her worried face.

Hesitantly she said, "Okay."

Another important commitment had come up, and she was juggling six kids in six different directions. I was thrilled with my mom, finally giving me some independence and letting me and my little sister take our scooters to our piano lesson. It was outside of our neighborhood, down a steep busy road, and into a separate neighborhood.

Back then "j-walking" felt like a pretty cool feat! You'd hurry across the street when no cars were around! I mean, I was twelve! Practically an adult! (Or so I thought.)

We made it to our piano lesson, then headed home shortly after. I remember my scooter wheels bumping up and down over the sidewalk lines with my little sister trailing behind.

I said a prayer in my mind and heart for safety. I knew I was old enough and brave enough to ride that far on such a busy road, but that feeling of hesitancy from my mom began to prod inside of me.

We began our journey up the steep hill. I was the older sister, after all, with my little sister, four years younger than me; so I was officially in charge and responsible for leading the way home. I looked ahead and realized that in the time since our journey down, some construction workers had closed off the sidewalk, and it was demolished for about fifteen feet. The only thing to do was *cross* the busy street *without a crosswalk.*

Well, I had j-walked before. It was easy. You just make sure no one is coming and go as fast as you can! And since I was the one in charge, I wanted to show my little sis how brave and cool I was.

So that's what I did.

I darted across the busy road, with my little sister trying her best to keep up with me. What I didn't realize was that the steep hill was actually made out of smaller hills that were just big enough to hide whatever might be coming in your direction; and on what I thought was a clear road, there was actually a rusty red car approaching us at forty-five miles per hour.

Now, where were *we* at this point? Smack dab center of the rusty car's lane.

My sister was about five feet behind me when the car veered onto the sidewalk to dodge us, spiraling out of control. The vehicle pressed on the brakes, carving smoky black tire marks into the road, turning so hard I thought it might roll. It crossed four lanes perpendicularly, managing to dodge oncoming traffic- and then came to a screeching halt.

When the car veered about five feet towards the sidewalk, that's exactly where my sister *had been*, trailing behind me. To this day, tears wallow in my eyes as I think of the danger I put her in; and if not danger, potential death. With the speed of the car and the position she was in, *she should have been hit* instantly.

I remember the horrified look of an onlooker- a woman who witnessed it all happen, and then asked if we were okay.

As we replay the event, my sister claims that I reached back and grabbed her, snatching her up by me; or perhaps that someone pushed her hard enough from behind to get her out of the way- just in time to dodge the car before completely running over her tiny body.

My perspective is: logically there's just no way my arm could reach that far.

He came for her. I truly believe that she is alive today because of the miracle of safety we needed that day.

3

He came for *me*, so that I could live a full life with my best friend.

And He came for *my mom* when she wasn't able to be there to protect us.

I believe God sends angels when moms can't be in two places at once.

CHAPTER 2

He Sent Mothers

"The love of a true mother comes nearer to being like the love of God than any other kind of love."
Joseph F. Smith

Growing up, I've always felt a closeness to Christ. I'm so grateful to my parents for creating the most beautiful childhood for us. I know that is not the case for many people.

As I grew into my motherhood and created a childhood for my own kids, I had the thought one day: "Why doesn't God send us to earth with weapons or some kind of protection; or maybe a *manual?* It's like sending your own kids off to war with nothing in hand and saying 'Best of luck!'"

After that silly (but very sincere) question, a thought

followed that stopped me in my tracks:

"He did. He sent Mothers."

After giving birth to four babies, and losing two, I've often joked with my husband that it should be the male's role to bring children into this world because it just feels like *too much* sometimes.

But as I've realized that mothers are the weapon that God gives His children as they go into our earthly war zone, I now know that I would never want to be robbed of that role.

"All that I am, or hope to be, I owe to my angel mother" are some of the famous words of Abraham Lincoln, about his mother, Nancy Lincoln, who died when he was nine-years-old. Though he knew her for such a short time, it is said that he remembered her for her warm affection and example.

So it has been for countless women and mothers throughout the world.

It makes me look at my role as a mother differently. It causes the role of any woman who nurtures children to feel different.

Neal A. Maxwell said, "When we return to our real home, it will be with the *mutual approbation* of those who reign in the *royal courts on high*. There, we will find beauty such as the mortal eye hath not seen; we will hear sounds surpassing music which mortal ear hath not heard. Could such a regal homecoming be possible, without the anticipatory arrangements of a Heavenly Mother?"

I believe in a God who has the power to send *anything* with His children as they enter into the world.

How incredible is it that His weapon of choice was-
and continues to be-

mothers.

"Have you ever wondered why prophets have taught
the doctrine of motherhood - and it is doctrine - again
and again? I have. I have thought long and hard
about the work of women of God. And I have wrestled
with what the doctrine of motherhood means for all of
us. This issue has driven me to my knees, to the
scriptures, and to the temple - all of which teach an
ennobling doctrine regarding our most crucial role as
women. It is a doctrine about which we must be clear
if we hope to stand 'steadfast and immovable'
regarding the issues that swirl around our gender. For
Satan has declared war on motherhood. He knows
that those who rock the cradle can rock his earthly
empire. And he knows that without righteous mothers
loving and leading the next generation, the
kingdom of God will fail.
When we understand the magnitude of
motherhood, it becomes clear why prophets have
been so protective of woman's most sacred role.
While we tend to equate motherhood solely with
maternity, in the Lord's language, the word mother
has layers of meaning. Of all the words they could
have chosen to define her role and her essence,
both God the Father and Adam called Eve 'the
mother of all living' - and they did so
before she ever bore a child.
Motherhood is more than bearing children, though
it is certainly that. It is the essence of who we are as
women. It defines our very identity, our divine stature
and nature, and the unique traits our Father gave us.

Sheri Dew

CHAPTER 3

In the Darkest Hour

"I am the light which shineth in darkness"
Doctrine and Covenants 6:21

I remember specifically where I was, standing in our two-bedroom apartment.

I had just had my first baby. He was only a few days old and he was suffering from severe acid reflux and colic. He was sobbing and I truly didn't know how to help him.

The thought, "Where's his mom? Who can I hand him off to?" crossed my mind pretty constantly. There was an overwhelming fear that flooded my body every time I thought, "I'm the mom."

There was no one else. It was just me. I was the mom. I felt the weight of the entire world on my shoulders. I couldn't send him back- this was forever now.

"I'm the mom, and I don't even know how to help him."

That thought was the start of a dark period of months for me. It was the thought that brought out some overwhelming anxieties deep within me that I never knew existed. I felt drenched in complete inadequacy. I wanted to be a mom all my life. What was my problem?

The days and weeks following were not the prettiest. A rocky start to breastfeeding triggered some painful infections. I began to feel complete dread every two to three hours, and big fat tears would fall onto my sweet baby's head. Every feeding lasted forty minutes as I cringed in pain and frustration.

Where was the mom who could take good care of him? I had no idea where she was, but I knew it wasn't me.

One day, my sister called and asked how I was doing. I was back in bed, per usual. Any chance I could get actually. It was cold and dark outside, and I was a "failing mom". I had lost every ounce of identity I ever had for myself.

She encouraged me to get some help and put on some jeans. (To this day, I believe that there's something about getting dressed that really does help. Thanks, Annalee!)

I remember needing a sense of control, because everything else felt so *out of control*. The one thing I felt like I could control was food. So I stopped eating.

I lost twenty-five pounds in two weeks. Having just had a baby, I was now smaller than I ever was in high school, barely weighing in at a hundred pounds. I had no desire to eat. This motherhood gig was too stressful for me. There was no time to take care of myself when I was putting another baby's colicky needs above my own.

I became obsessive in how I mothered. I worried about every little thing, and I didn't have enough sleep to think clearly (which I think most moms can relate to).

Dark days seemed to last longer, and a monster in my mind kept crawling in.

With postpartum depression, it's common to have intrusive thoughts. And when I say that I had obsessive, intrusive thoughts, I want you to think of a fly that buzzes in your ear over and over again, but you can't do anything to get it out.

It was out of my control which became so scary for my new-mom self. Thoughts of harming my baby or myself replayed in my head over and over, followed by the feeling of complete guilt and shame. I hid the knives in the kitchen in fear of what I was capable of. I would sing hymns every time a dark thought crossed my mind. It was like a war zone in my head:

"It would probably be better for EVERYONE if you just killed yourself."

"I am a child of God."

"But it would be so easy and you wouldn't have to do this anymore."

"I am a child of God."

"The world is better off without you."

"I am a child of a God."

"You aren't any good at this anyway and he deserves a better mom. You could even just kill everyone so they could be with you anywhere else but here."

"I AM A CHILD OF GOD!"

Was I crazy? I didn't want my husband to know, because I thought for sure he would up-and-leave me. I mean, who would want to be married to a girl who was a total failure at being a mom, plus a monster who has thoughts of killing her family and herself?

I silently suffered for a while, gulping down my own nothingness and trying to act like I had it together. It was one of the times in my life where I literally gave it my all. Physically, mentally, emotionally, spiritually; yet it was never enough. I'd never felt so low before.

At a family gathering a sweet cousin asked how I was *really* doing and it was like she had lifted up the lid of a can of worms I was suffocating in. Could she truly understand *why* I was crazy?

She was my safe place that night, and offered some incredible advice: Talk to my husband and get some help.

That night I told Shey (my husband) on our drive home. To my surprise, he didn't just up-and-leave! In fact, he did the complete opposite. I remember feeling so relieved. I was baffled that he still wanted to be married to me. And I didn't even know who "me" was.

During my battle against the thick darkness of postpartum depression, I hit a breaking point. Shey had to go back to work, and I had to be strong, but I couldn't muster any strength in my bones. I was exhausted; and taking care of another human's needs twenty-four-seven had me questioning if I was truly cut out for this.

I felt like maybe this was the end for me.

One night specifically, Shey was at work and my baby was asleep in his crib. I hadn't been eating much in weeks because of my stress levels, and that night was no different. I had finally gotten my baby to fall asleep, and I went to eat a few carrots that felt so hard to swallow.

You know that lump in your throat that comes when you know you have to have a hard conversation? I *constantly* felt that. I felt guilty for taking time to even nourish my own body- when I needed to take care of someone else who would probably be awake in the next twenty minutes.

I remember standing in my living room with my plate of carrots, just feeling so weak. I took one bite before I found myself collapsed onto the ground. I blacked out and the plate fell to the ground. I was a useless, pathetic mess.

In my mind, I truly thought I might die of inadequacy and depression.

I blacked out. The next thing I remember is laying there and looking up.

I spotted our most beautiful picture of the Savior in our hallway, and at that moment I said out loud, "Am I going to die?"

I cried, knowing that someone might be actually listening.

And *He* was.

I managed to get back up that night. Seeing that picture of Christ gave me the strength I needed when I felt completely alone.

I called a nurse and told her what was going on. She could sense the desperation in my voice and immediately offered me the help I needed.

It took a good while to return to "normal" but I truly don't know if I would have been able to peel myself up off of the ground that night without the knowledge that *someone had suffered for me.*

He knew exactly how I felt. *He* knew the demons I was facing.

He was there in my literal darkest hour. *He* came for me.

Since then, I've shared this story to thousands, hoping to at least help *one* mom who might feel the same way I did. I wanted to create a safe place for women to turn, just like I had felt with my cousin, and to offer tools like therapy, meditation, movement classes, and more- in addition to getting medical help.

In the year 2020, I founded ANYA which means "Mama" in Hungarian, and stands for A New You Again. ANYA was created to help women and mothers with their mental health: prenatal, postpartum, and beyond. If you are struggling, or know of another mama who is, please don't suffer alone!

Visit www.anewyouagain.com

"They that wait upon the Lord shall renew their strength; they shall mount up with wings as eagles; they shall run, and not be weary; and they shall walk, and not faint."

Isaiah 40:31

CHAPTER 4

He Believes in the Rebuild

"Jesus specializes in the seemingly impossible. He came here to make the impossible possible, the irredeemable redeemable, to heal the unhealable, to right the un-rightable, to promise the un-promisable. And He's really good at it. In fact, He's perfect at it."
Elder Patrick Kearon

Last year, I had surgery on my ankle. The purpose was to break my already-weak joint and put it back together. To rebuild it so it could be stronger.

What I learned through this season of life is that *God loves weak and broken things.*

The process of Kintsugi is so fascinating to me. It's a Japanese art of putting broken pottery pieces back together using gold. The idea behind it is that it *embraces* the flaws, broken pieces and imperfections of the pottery, while building a stronger and more beautiful piece of art.

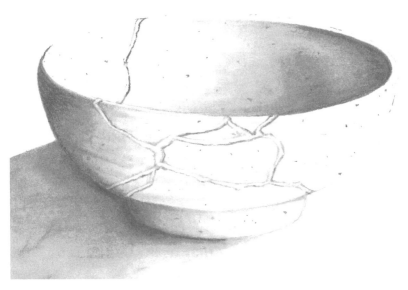

"If you are lonely, please know you can find comfort. If you are discouraged, please know you can find hope. If you are poor in spirit, please know you can be strengthened. If you feel you are broken, please know you can be mended."

Elder Jeffrey R. Holland

I've often thought of myself as a broken piece of pottery: sometimes too shattered to even attempt to fix, but I have found that when we bring our broken pieces to Christ, *He is what turns our brokenness into something beautiful.* It's the broken cracks that allow His light to shine in.

I think the hardest part of "rebuilding" is the process that happens after the breaking and deconstructing.

15

"That which is of God is light; and he that receiveth light, and continueth in God, receiveth more light; and that light groweth brighter and brighter until the perfect day"

Doctrine and Covenants 50:24

It's the time and empty space that happens after you lose someone.

It's the waiting game when you're trying to grow your family.

It's the healing inbetween.

It's the period of time that tests you the most and feels the longest.

After ankle surgery with four small kids, one being a baby that couldn't walk on her own, I started to rebuild physically and emotionally. It was quite a process and my mental health got the best of me.

I had an infection during the healing process and experienced septic symptoms. I remember saying goodbye to my babies before heading off to the Emergency Room, truly believing it was my last time seeing them. Anxiety is such a beast sometimes, isn't it?

I remember the day finally came where I had finally healed enough to walk. I allowed God and meditation to be a part of my healing, and I'm so grateful for that. I got a little stronger everyday and I remember crying happy tears when I could do small jumps, side-to-side.

The reward of the "rebuild" is that you become far

greater than you ever were before. Rebuilding and reconstructing takes work, *but you are worth fighting for!*

Every effort you do, adds to your rebuild. Even the smallest things count.

"Behold, I have graven thee upon the palms of my hands; thy walls are continually before Me."

Isaiah 49:16

What are you rebuilding right now? Maybe it's not your ankle, but maybe it's a marriage. A relationship. Your faith. Your home. Yourself after trauma. Your heart.

Being cracked or broken is the very thing that allows light to come through. It's the starting line to a rebuild. It's the thing that allows us to become so much greater than we ever have been before. You are never too broken or too far gone.

God believes in the rebuild.

"Therefore if any man be in Christ, he is a new creature: cold things have passed away; behold, all things have become new."

2 Corinthians 5:17

CHAPTER 5

Be Not Afraid, Only Believe

"We love him, because he first loved us."
1 John 4:19

I think everyone should have a "faith crisis." Can I say that?

I don't mean that as a bold or blanket statement, but when we question our very beliefs and allow ourselves to strip away all that we've ever learned and take our questions and hard conversations to God, I believe we can come out stronger than we were before. Just like a rebuild.

He takes our weaknesses and He makes them our strengths; but it's *our* job to come to Him. Too often we question, and then we listen to voices on both sides of the spectrum, and it makes our weak points weaker.

When we turn to He who has all the answers and *cancel the outside noise,* this is when we can find understanding and clarity.

The last two years, I've done a lot of soul searching;

mostly about my own beliefs that I was born and raised in: The Church of Jesus Christ of Latter Day Saints. To be honest, a lot of doubts crept in. We live in a time where it's praised (or so it feels) to "leave the norm" and walk away from religion.

I would be lying if I said all of these voices had not made me question.

After the Covid-19 pandemic, there was a specific Sunday where we started gathering at church in person, and I remember vividly thinking about how easy it would be to just…not go back.

With little kids - including a baby - I didn't see the purpose of it and the thought alone made me exhausted. I felt like I would have more spiritual experiences alone, than I would at church; so what was the point in going?

So, I didn't go.

A few months prior to this, Shey had been called as the Bishop of our congregation- just a mere *nine days* after our fourth baby was born. We were, and still are, very young for this role.

I felt a lot of bitterness toward God because of this calling. I felt like He took my husband away when He knew my history with postpartum depression, and I was already feeling it come on. I was not in a good state of mind, and people with strong testimonies all felt so self-righteous to me, like they hadn't ever had a hard time. I fell into "victim land" pretty quickly.

I just couldn't hear the music of the gospel anymore.

It was like watching a room full of people, dancing and laughing to music that I couldn't hear. It was a devastating feeling since the music of the gospel had been such a huge part of my identity and I couldn't recognize it anymore.

During that very same time, a neighbor offered to take my kids to church. When they'd knock on the door on Sunday mornings to help finish tying their shoes, my kids would say, "Mom the angels are here to pick us up!"

That neighbor and my kids are literally the only reason why I started to go back to church again. At first it was just so my kids could go to Primary, and I would grin-and-bear-it. There was also the fact that Shey was the Bishop, so I'd go to support him.

Little by little, I realized that I don't go to church for peace- I'm usually chasing kids the whole time, anyway!

I don't go for the social aspect because let's be honest- I'd rather stay in my pjs!

This whole time, I've tried to see what the church can do for ME. What would *I* get out of it? I've since realized that I don't go to church for myself; and I actually don't go for others either.

I go for Him.

I go for Jesus Christ. I go because He's asked me to. I go because I believe Him when he promises protection. No more halfsies for me. I want to be ALL IN! To wear my garments when it's not convenient, to make sure I'm there for the sacrament- even when my kids are having meltdowns; and to have a foundation for my kids to thrive in when the world feels heavy.

So count me in. He chose us.

And now I choose Him.

CHAPTER 6

Because She Can

"Let [sisterly] love continue. Be not forgetful to entertain strangers: for thereby somehave entertained angels unawares."
Hebrews 13:1-2

I recently opened up about my faith journey on a podcast (The Minivan Mamas Podcast), and a sweet friend and social media follower was listening and prayerfully asked, "Why did she become the Bishop's wife with a nine-day-old baby?" and the words, "Because she can!" came to her mind.

She reached out and shared those words with me on a day that was full of stress, motherhood exhaustion, and a day where I wanted to throw in the towel.

When you feel hopeful or positive about someone, don't hesitate sharing it with them!

He came to me -*through her*- that day.

We have the opportunity to be angels in the lives of others if we just prayerfully ask each day, "Who can I serve? Who needs me today? Please let me be an instrument in Thy hands."

I've been on both the giving and receiving end of the Lord's errand, and it's a beautiful work to be a part of.

My deepest hope is that if *you* ever question your own strength on your own hard days, or throughout the hard tasks that God sometimes asks of you, I hope that those same words will come to your mind about *you:*

"Because she can."

CHAPTER 7

Healing in His Wings

"Be faithful in Christ; and may not the things which I have written grieve thee, to weigh thee down unto death; but may Christ lift thee up, and may his sufferings and death, and the showing his body unto our fathers, and his mercy and long-suffering, and the hope of his glory and of eternal life, rest in your mind forever."
Moroni 9:25

I was twelve when I had my first surgery: two inguinal hernias and a mole was being removed off my back. Nothing too crazy, but for a twelve-year-old it felt like a lot to know I would be doubled over in pain when I walked to the bathroom throughout the healing process.

When I went in for the surgery, I wrote "yes"- opting in for them to slice me open. Sounds dramatic, I know. I've thought about this experience and how we opt-in to the hard stuff life gives us for what will ultimately be for our good.

We said "yes" to the crappy stuff before we even got

here because we knew it would give us a chance to bring us to the surgeon; our Master Healer.

If we could strip our egos and bodies away, I think we'd see souls who long to be with Him; souls who are willing to go through anything to be with Him.

Another name for Savior is *rock*. Maybe He is who we need at rock bottom.

If I've learned anything in my thirty-four years of life, it's that healing is constant. We heal from scraped knees, broken hearts, broken bones, surgeries, diseases -the list goes on- up until the complete healing: death.

"We are troubled on every side, yet not distressed; we are perplexed, but not in despair; Persecuted, but not forsaken; cast down, but not destroyed; Always bearing about in the body the dying of the Lord Jesus, that the life also of Jesus might be made manifest in our body.

2 Corinthians 4:8-10

God has asked us to opt-in so that He can fully heal us; and even though healing is usually pretty messy, once we're all stitched up, the scars tell the story of us finding Him and being healed by Him.

And I think there's something beautiful about that.

"But unto you that fear my name shall the Sun of righteousness arise with healing in his wings"

Malachi 4:2

CHAPTER 8

Mister Rogers

"If ye fulfill the royal law according to the scripture, Thou shalt love thy neighbor as thyself, ye do well."
James 2:8

I used to think Fred Rogers was an interesting fella, but after watching a movie about him I've become completely captivated by him. The way he shifts his focus away from his own agenda to whoever he's with, is remarkable to me. He leaves his whole world at the door, and whoever he's with becomes everything to him- especially if they seem a little "broken".

One day, I had an interesting experience. I was getting my nails done, and the guy who was doing mine stepped outside for a smoking break before coming back in to work on my fingernails. If I'm being completely honest, I was grossed out a little, and I hate the smell of smoke. I had negative thoughts about how unprofessional he seemed as he came back in with a cigarette behind his ear and offered a few smoky coughs in my face. I cringed a little as I put my hands up for him to touch and to work on. I also happen to be an extreme germaphobe so that didn't help in this case.

A few seconds went by in a swirl of judgment, and I thought, "No, I'm gonna *Mister Rogers* this moment!"

I started to get to know this guy! His story. His background. I put my own agenda aside, and focused on his. He was divorced, and lived with his brother in Las Vegas, and would travel hours to work at this salon. He had two beautiful girls. He was a devout Buddhist. He was moving to Hawaii the very next week to go back to island life because Vegas wasn't for him. He told me how he had a hard time believing anything he couldn't see, but tried his best to "live right anyway."

We sat for a while, and instead of trying to relate my own life to him or think of how to respond, I just listened. I shifted the conversation back to him every time. I wanted to know his worries and what he was dealing with. I wanted to know how he saw the world.

I quickly learned to love this Vietnamese smoker who was working on my manicure. It was such a crazy social experiment that I hope to continue to do.

I can't help but see some parallels here.

I believe Christ, though probably the one with THE most important agenda, was the one who left it at the door the second he sat down with people. He was the type who allowed them to stay awhile. His focus was completely on them. He loved the "broken and smoky" people. He got to know them, and love them.

I'm reminded of a quote by one of my heroes,

Mother Theresa, who was asked if she always thought, "What would Jesus do?" when she served people.

Her response was, "No, I look at each person and ask, 'What if that were Jesus?'"

I think of that often. What friendships have I missed out on because I was too caught up in my own life and schedule? What promptings have I missed because of the need to be busy?

I hope to *Mister Rodgers* more in my life. I hope to find more of Christ in other people. I hope when He needs me to be an instrument in His hands in some way, that I'm willing; and that He'll trust me.

CHAPTER 9

Don't Give Up

"If I was sunk in the lowest pit of Nova Scotia and all the Rocky Mountains piled on top of me, I ought not to be discouraged, but hang on, exercise faith, and keep up good courage and I should come out on the top of the heap at last."
Joseph Smith, just a few days before being martyred.

Where do you feel like Christ has come to you? Where do you feel him most?

Is it your kitchen floor? When you're alone in the shower, and have specific thoughts come to mind? In your closet? Outside in nature? While you do the dishes?

I've developed a practice through the years that has helped me to feel Him daily. The times we feel His distance are usually the times we are actually distancing ourselves from Him, rather than Him distancing Himself from us.

The best thing I've done for myself and my relationship with Him is to set an appointment every day to be with Him. Whether it ends up being five minutes or two hours, it doesn't really matter. What matters is *my heart* while I'm there.

28

There have been days where my prayers have simply been, "Help me to try again tomorrow. In the name of Jesus Christ, Amen."

There are also days where deep conversations happen and He has inspired me to do specific things, like to write this book!

One experience I fall back on a lot is asking Him *how he feels about me,* and pausing long enough for Him to let me know.

I'm a big believer in stillness and meditation. It is my favorite tool for my anxiety and depression because it's the door to Him. I believe if we ask with pure intent *how He feels about us,* that this prayer will never go unanswered.

He believes in women. He believes in YOU.

He needs more women and mothers to be a force for good. *He needs you!*

When you begin to learn how God truly feels about you and that He isn't cursing you and making your life worse, it helps you to tap into your divine potential and discover gifts you never knew you had!

The biggest life-lesson I've learned from my young adult experience, is that when you don't give up on God He never gives up on you. His love is absolute.

"For I am persuaded, that neither death, nor life, nor angels, nor principalities, nor powers, nor things present, nor things to come, Nor height, nor depth, nor any other creature, shall be able to separate us from the love of God, which is in Christ Jesus our Lord."

Romans 8: 38-39

In my recent years, I've come to learn that even *when you do* give up on Him, He *still* doesn't ever give up on you. And he'll patiently wait for us to come back with open arms. How wonderful is our God! His love is pure, divine and eternal.

"Never give up—however deep the wounds of your soul, whatever their source, wherever or whenever they happen, and however short or long they persist, you are not meant to perish spiritually. Look forward. Your troubles and sorrows are very real, but they will not last forever. Your dark night will pass, because 'the Son [did rise] with healing in his wings.' You may be exhausted, but don't ever give up."

Elder Neil L. Andersen

"Don't give up. You keep walking. You keep trying. There is help and happiness ahead—a lot of it—30 years of it now, and still counting. You keep your chin up. It will be alright in the end. Trust God and believe in good things to come." We all have times when we want to give up. But the gospel of Jesus Christ helps us know that things will always get better."

Elder Jeffrey R. Holland

CHAPTER 10

When He Doesn't Come

When you are going through difficulty and wonder where God is, remember that the teacher is always quiet during the test.
Anonymous

Have you ever had a time in your life where you felt like He *hasn't* come for you? Maybe you've begged and pleaded and felt, nothing? We talk of all of this love that God has for us, but what about the times when we feel abandoned and deserted?

It makes me think of my five-year-old. She was so nervous to start school this year. Her social anxiety was heartbreaking to watch. Any time she'd be around someone she didn't know, she wouldn't speak. She'd hide behind me and start to cry. It got to the point where I just wanted to keep her home from everything, because it was exhausting to try and get her to do new things.

We'd put her in soccer and the only way she'd participate was if we'd run on the field right next to her, basically tripping over each other's feet with our arms wrapped around each other!

Then the first day of Kindergarten came.

I became more nervous for her because I didn't know how we would all survive. She was so scared, and quite frankly -and secretly- I was too.

We sent her anyway. It was one of those things where you know you are supposed to do something, but you really don't want to; and it was that way for *all of us*.

Holding back the tears, she showed up.

She wouldn't talk to anyone at first, but after a summer full of tears surrounding this, she still showed up on that first day. I couldn't stop thinking about her, and couldn't wait to hold her and to tell her how proud I was of her.

She showed up -scared and alone. And in her world, this was a huge deal. I couldn't be with her. I couldn't come to save the day. As much as I wanted to keep her home and not have to enter into the world, deep down I knew this was going to be good for her.

And guess what? She went the next day, and then the day after, and the day after that!

The confidence she has been able to build is unreal. She actually talks to her teacher. She made friends, and now she loves school so much that she skips off to her class every morning with a big "goodbye" wave to me as she hops out of the car. She is thriving!

It makes me wonder how God felt when He first sent us off to "Kindergarten."

A world that was new to us.

I wonder if He felt anxious for us but knew the outcome would benefit our souls -so He did it anyway. And the times where we feel like He's not around, maybe he actually is! Maybe He's thinking of us non-stop and can't wait to hold us and tell us how proud He is of us after our first day!

Maybe He doesn't desert us, but rather gives us the opportunity to be scared- and do it anyway so that we can become who we are supposed to be.

My little Kindergartner happened to also be a NICU baby (Which I mention later in this book).

There was a specific day where they had to put an IV in her tiny little head. I held her hand for as long as I could before the pain in my heart physically became too much to bear.

I had to step to the side and stand behind the curtain wall.

Can you imagine how our Father in Heaven felt when He had to watch Jesus Christ suffer without stepping in?

More than the pain of the broken heart of a parent-He must have felt behind the curtain of clouds. However, He saw the bigger picture. He knew what needed to happen and allowed space- not of abandonment- but a space of exponential growth that could not happen any other way.

I think if we could see the bigger picture, we would have a greater appreciation for the space that He offers, and find gratitude for who we are becoming when God doesn't swoop in and save the day, take it away from us, or let us stay home from Kindergarten!

"I ask you, what father and mother could stand by and listen to the cry of their children in distress ... and not render assistance? I have heard of mothers throwing themselves into raging streams when they could not swim a stroke to save their drowning children, [I have heard of fathers] rushing into burning buildings to rescue those whom they loved. In the same way, God rushes to our aid when we call on him. In that hour I think I can see our dear Father behind the veil looking upon these dying struggles until even he could not endure it any longer; and, like the mother who bids farewell to her dying child, has to be taken out of the room, so as not to look upon the last struggles, as he bowed his head, and hid in some part of his universe, his great heart almost breaking for the love that he had for his Son."

Elder Melvin J. Ballard

CHAPTER 11

The Power of the Word AND

"And the peace of God, which passeth all understanding, shall keep your hearts and minds through Christ Jesus."
Philippians 4:6-7

We waited two years after our first baby to start trying for our next.

I was thrilled to find out that we got pregnant pretty quickly and it was all "working out as planned"- until it wasn't.

I went in for my eight-week appointment and took my two-year-old with me, to check on our baby. I was so thrilled to see a tiny baby and a heartbeat!

They handed us ultrasound pictures of our baby and I remember taking pictures of our two-year-old holding the ultrasounds, celebrating quietly in the hallway, waiting for our doctor to come talk with us about how exciting this all was!

"Your baby has an eighty percent chance of miscarrying." He said.

The baby's heart rate wasn't high enough.

"But twenty percent? I can work with that! I can put my faith in this and get a miracle baby here!" I thought.

I put myself on bedrest for the next four weeks just to help my chances, but deep down I knew.

I had angels come in the form of friends, flowers, cards, and donuts. I felt lucky to have the support. Each week we'd check on the baby, and each week the heartbeat would get slower and slower. I grew a special bond with this baby that I can't fully describe. I had never watched someone die, but watching my baby slowly die over the span of four weeks completely broke my heart.

Twelve weeks came, and I was still pregnant. I went to see where the heart rate was -and this time- there wasn't one. I remember the ultrasound tech was so kind and full of sympathy, but that day I truly felt held by a Higher Power.

I said "Thank you," and excused myself to the restroom where I offered up a prayer of gratitude for the time I got to be with this baby.

It was almost as if I was holding this infant and passing them off to Heavenly Father for Him to take over. I did my part.

I will always remember the peace I felt as I knelt on that sanitized bathroom floor. It was a sacred place for me. This was the first time I realized the power of the word *AND*.

How you can feel sorrow *AND* peace at the same time.

It's a gift God gives to all of us, like in nature when

it rains *and* the sun is shining at the same time (my favorite nature phenomenon). Two feelings can coexist. It can be beautiful *and* painful.

Shortly after that, we got pregnant again! I couldn't believe it, but it was short-lived for just seven weeks.

I could get pregnant quickly, but my body couldn't hold onto my babies.

We were sent to an infertility specialist where we were told we wouldn't be able to have babies without going through the process of IVF. During this time, life felt a little bit dark.

Okay- a LOT bit dark. Almost as if I lived in a world of gray. And I craved color.

I remember taking my two-year-old all over Dallas, Texas, where we lived, to find any kind of color we could! We would find bright yellow walls and take pictures of them.

I started a hashtag- #mysunshinelist- on my Instagram, where I would list all of the little things I was grateful for! Most of those posts were written behind magnifying tears and a broken heart, but I craved to feel any kind of light and color that I could find.

Some of those lists included meeting new neighbors who seemed genuine, early morning bike rides, sharing a slice of Costco pizza, catching up on laundry, squeezing lemons in ice-water, homemade popsicles, two-year-old snuggles, and big southern storms.

Texas has the most incredible rainstorms- thunder that shakes your whole house, and lightning that lights up the entire sky. When we first moved to Texas, I was terrified of tornadoes, but when I kept losing my babies, the storms were what made me feel *alive*. It would rain so hard that it felt like you were taking a shower. Those were the best kind!

When the gutters would turn into rivers and you'd get drenched after taking one step outside, it wouldn't matter if I had just washed my hair! I would instantly run and grab our toddler and take him out to dance in the rain with me!

The rain is where I felt healing. It's what made me feel alive and free. It's where I felt His love and almost an acknowledgment of my broken heart. To this day, my little guy still loves to dance in the rain!

During that time, I decided to keep fighting for our family. I went to another specialist who told me that my chances of having a healthy baby on my own were seventy percent- quite different from what previous doctors had told me! This doctor took a chance on me. And I believed in him. I knew he could help me. We got pregnant on our own and I was able to carry her to thirty-seven weeks and deliver her safely.

This baby was so loved by doctors, nurses, family, and friends before she was even born because they all knew what it took to get her here! I even had neighbors making quilts with her name on it; which you might've guessed her middle name by now:

Rain.

Those years felt really dark, but I knew the Savior stayed close to me. He knew my heart longed for babies and was broken.

And yet there were glimpses of light in the form of

people's smiles, love notes, and peace. Life sometimes feels heart-wrenching and I think that in those moments, He carries us.

It can rain *and* shine. You can feel grief *and* peace, heartache *and* hope, sadness *and* love. They can coexist. And there's something really beautiful about that.

CHAPTER 12

When It's Fragile

"Therefore, fear not, little a flock; do good; let
earth and hell combine against you, for if ye
are built upon my rock, they cannot prevail. Behold, I
do not condemn you; go your ways and sin no more;
perform with soberness the work which I have
commanded you. Look unto me in every thought;
doubt not, fear not. Behold the wounds which
pierced my side, and also the prints of the nails in my
hands and feet; be faithful, keep my commandments,
and ye shall inherit the kingdom of heaven. Amen."
Doctrine and Covenants 6:34-37

My "Rainy girl" was born at thirty-seven weeks. I have Factor V, which is a blood-clotting issue and they watched it closely.

I did blood-thinning shots everyday, and my belly would be covered in hematomas, but I was proud of the work I could do and grateful to get her here.

The day she was born was one of the best days of

my life. There is something about a rainbow baby that brings in a whole new perspective, almost as if your gratitude and love for this baby is magnified by ten!

After I gave birth, I got to hold her for a little bit, but she wasn't crying very much. Her nostrils were flaring and the nurses were trying to rub her down to get her to cry more. Our sweet little rainbow was whisked away to the NICU to get more support.

Shortly after, I remember my legs still in the stirrups and my doctor calling for backup. My doctor was the best of the best, who else would she need? And *WHY?*

Next thing I knew, I had multiple doctor's arms up inside me up to their elbows.

My placenta had ruptured and I was hemorrhaging.

I ended up needing two blood transfusions, but if I'm being completely honest, I was still in the clouds, knowing my rainbow baby was here.

I was thrilled to be alive and in such good hands.

NICU life was a new experience for us. I'm an empath by nature and to be on a hospital floor with so many suffering babies, my heart would break every single day with what I witnessed.

It was such a sacred and beautiful experience and I felt the presence of angels surrounding each baby. I was impressed to hear that the nurses would pray over their babies every morning. It was a sacred place.

Having to leave my baby at the hospital and be separated felt so wrong. I would come back every single day. They would have to put an IV in her head because her arm and hand were just too little. My mama heart could hardly stand it and felt depleted from praying, nursing, pumping, crying, and praying some more.

My angel during our NICU experience came in the form of a dear friend who sent this text:

"Say a prayer before you go into the NICU and ask to witness miracles and see your blessings and I promise you, you will see with such clarity it will change you. The NICU nurses are still angels as far as I'm concerned, and I loved spending time getting to know them and why they chose to work there. NICU gets a bad stigma but I think it should be changed to a badge of honor. Not everyone gets to experience the NICU, and the incredible miracles and blessings that come through there. Congratulations mama. You've been selected- and what a beautiful journey it is. You were picked because YOU and Baby Girl are strong enough, and will come out on top like champions. Wear your NICU mama badge with pride, and look for the beauty all around you..."

I'm so grateful for our days spent at the NICU and the day we were able to take her home. My heart ached for the babies who spent a long time there and broken for the mamas who had to give their child back to heaven.

When life becomes fragile, it adds a layer to your perspective on life and our need for the Savior. We need him. Every hour.

CHAPTER 13

Your Gain is Mine

"And he shall go forth, suffering pains and afflictions and temptations of every kind; and this that the word might be fulfilled which saith he will take upon him the pains and the sicknesses of his people. And he will take upon him death, that he may loose the bands of death which bind his people; and he will take upon him their infirmities, that his bowels may be filled with mercy, according to the flesh, that he may know according to the flesh how to succor his people according to their infirmities."
Alma 7:11-12

Christ has come to me in the form of words. Sometimes from other people.

During my years of pregnancy and miscarriages, there was one specific time where I had gotten pregnant and we had become best friends with a couple who had been trying for years as well. I remember the guilt I felt and the tears that welled up in my eyes as I told her I was pregnant, almost apologetically.

"Your gain is our gain." was their response.

44

I was dumbfounded. My gain was theirs? It was a new concept for me.

Especially when you are hurting and yearning for your own rainbow and someone else gets one, it's easy to fall into a victim trap; but their response has changed my life. After that incident, I ended up losing that baby and I learned the meaning of "your loss is ours" too.

It goes both ways and what a beautiful way to mourn with those that mourn when we can truly sit in it with them.

I believe that we are here to not just learn about the savior, but to *feel* as he did too. I've often thought that He suffered so that He could understand us, and we have to sometimes suffer in our lives -to better understand Him. When we feel like no one understands, there is one that can step forward and that can say,

"I understand."

CHAPTER 14

Make it Sacred

"That which cometh from above is sacred, and must be
spoken with care, and by constraint of the Spirit"
Doctrine and Covenants 63:64

We had a curtain in our kitchen that had been broken for a few months.

We just never had the time or energy to fix it between our busy schedules.

And so it hung there, crooked with one side on and the other side off, and the bar hanging from one side -just dangling!

I decided one night I was just going to take a few minutes to fix it up real quick. I grabbed the ladder and some power tools and within a few minutes it was fixed and looking so much better. I took a step back and was in awe at how putting even just a little loving effort into something made such a difference!

"Make it sacred." came to my mind as I looked at this corner of our home.

So I didn't stop there! I started wiping off every sticky surface and turning this little corner into something that was cared for and a beautiful place to gather our family for dinner.

The phrase "make it sacred" has stuck with me.

When I do laundry. When I clean the house. When I read to my kids books on repeat, when I'm up at night, feeding my baby in the moonlight.

When we make something sacred, it gives purpose and meaning to us. It brings value to the very thing we are making sacred. It makes it special.

Any mundane task can turn into something meaningful if we only decide to make it sacred. By doing so, it prepares and allows a special feeling in the home. A place where He can come.

CHAPTER 15

You're Going to Be Okay!

"Peace I leave with you, my peace I give unto you: not as the world giveth, give I unto you. Let not your heart be troubled, neither let it be afraid"
John 14:26-27

Motherhood, for me, is a divine partnership with God. Some people call it motherly instinct. I call it a divine partnership. I *need* him. Every day. Some days, every hour, even every minute.

As a new mom, my anxiety would be through the roof, with so many different things:

"Is my baby breathing?"

"Are they sick enough to take to the ER?"

"Do I need to check up on them every few hours of the night?"

"What is this rash?"

Oh, how the list goes on for the worries of a mother's heart! I've learned something in my divine partnership with God that has saved my mama heart and mind. It's helped with my anxiety and helps me function:

If I have a worried thought, I allow myself to become fully immersed in the present moment. Oftentimes, this happens as I peek at my kids from the doorway as they're sleeping, or when I'm soothing them when they're sick.

I close my eyes and allow my brain to go inward and upward. I try to be as present as possible, focusing on my breath and being still. Once I've paused long enough to be in the present moment, I ask, "Are they going to be okay?" and then I pause and listen for the first answer that comes to my mind and heart.

I did this a lot when the pandemic hit in 2020 and caused a lot of panic.

I write this, knowing that some situations truly don't feel like they're going to be okay. Maybe we're losing a loved one or suffering through something that seems to be too much.

It's okay to not be okay, and to sit in that emotion for as long as you need; but in the eternal scheme of things, everything really is going to be okay. When we have overwhelming fear, *He is our good news.*

When we have debilitating anxiety, *He is our peace.*

When we are crawling through the pits of depression, *He is our light.*

And you my friend, no matter what you are facing, because of Him,

you are going to be okay.

As you read these accounts of the Savior coming to the following women, I hope you are able to relate it to your own life as you ponder the times you have felt Him.

I hope it encourages you to be an instrument in His hands, and gives you hope to continue looking for evidence of Him.

My hope is that you start to see Him in your life every day even in seemingly small ways. And that as you come to know Him, you will notice how often He comes to -and for- you.

"Be a woman of Christ. Cherish your esteemed place in the sight of God. He needs you. This church needs you. The world needs you. A woman's abiding trust in God and unfailing devotion to things of the Spirit have always been an anchor when the wind and the waves of life were fiercest."

Elder Jeffrey R. Holland

Part 2:

He Came For HER: A Collection of Stories from Modern-Day Women

"The complexities of this life at times tend to be very dehumanizing and overwhelming. Some have so much, while others struggle with so very little. Some faithful women have been denied that which is at the very center of their souls. In the eternal plan, no blessing will be kept from the faithful. No woman should question how the Savior values womanhood. The grieving Mary Magdalene was the first to visit the sepulcher after the Crucifixion, and when she saw that the stone had been rolled away and that the tomb was empty...Mary stayed. There, she was honored to be the first mortal to see the risen Lord. After He said, "Woman, why weepest thou?"...To the question "Woman, why weepest thou?" I testify of the great atoning sacrifice and breaking of the bonds of death by the Lord Jesus Christ, which shall indeed wipe away our tears."

James E. Faust

BY KARILEE OLSEN

Angel in the Airport

The year my husband went to law school, we traveled home to Utah for the Christmas holiday. When the holidays ended, it was time to head back home to Washington.

I was three months pregnant, and sick as could be. We boarded a plane and planned to land in Portland Oregon. As we approached the airport, we ended up having to circle in the air for an hour because of the fog.

We finally landed, and what was supposed to be a short delay, turned into hours of waiting. Then we found our flight was canceled. We were stuck in the airport with three boxes of Christmas gifts and four pieces of luggage, my toddler, and my pregnant belly.

My daughter wasn't feeling well. My husband told me to stay right where I was and he would go and find out what to do and how to get home.

After a few minutes I pulled all of my stuff over to the bank of phones. I decided to call a relative to see if he could help us.

As I was talking to him, I could smell a terrible smell and I looked down at my daughter who was standing in a puddle of sick stomach diarrhea. She was covered. Her shoes and socks were filled and her pants were soaked. I had no other choice than to leave all of our things in the middle of the airport and take her to the restroom to clean her up. I opened the suitcase and found clean clothes and diapers for my little girl.

When we got into the restroom, I started to take off her clothes.

A young woman (My Guardian Angel) had followed me in and suggested I use the changing table. My daughter was such a mess I just stuck her in the sink to clean her off.

The young woman then picked up all of her soiled clothes and rinsed them out in the toilet. She told me she would be right back. She then left and went and found a janitor's closet to find a plastic bag to put all of the wet clothes in.

When she came back, she cleaned off all of the counters around me and wished me a Happy New Year. I had finished dressing my little girl and gathered up all of my stuff. I followed this sweet person out of the bathroom to thank her. I was just a few seconds behind her. When I went out into the hallway, it was empty. She was nowhere to be found in either direction.

I was so grateful to this young woman that had seen my need and jumped in to help me. I think it was divine intervention and the Lord had sent me a guardian angel to help me in a desperate time. I wish I could find this young woman and tell her how much her act of kindness helped me. I went back to my huge pile of belongings, and my husband eventually came back to help us.

We were able to get on a bus and make it home after 12 hours of traveling from Salt Lake City! I am so grateful to a Father in Heaven that can see our needs and who sends others to help us. What a great love he has for us.

BY CAROL BUNKER

The Virgin River

On Saturday, August 29, 1998, we were living in Orem, Utah. My husband, Gary, and I were planning to attend a funeral for his uncle in Las Vegas, Nevada. We knew we would have to leave early that morning to arrive at the funeral on time. Before leaving we offered a prayer, asking Heavenly Father to bless us on this quick trip.

Gary drove from Orem to St. George, while I tried to sleep in the passenger seat. In Saint George, he asked me if I could drive for a while because he was feeling tired. As I was driving, I was enjoying the beautiful scenery of the Virgin Narrows. All at once I was jerked awake as we were going off the road and down the Narrows at freeway speed, launching a life-threatening accident with a high probability of serious injury, or even death for each of us. Gary also awoke as we traveled across the Narrows for about fifty feet. A huge semi-truck, going in the opposite direction, blew its horn, in an effort, to warn us.

We were now at the mercy of the rocky Virgin Narrows terrain. Thankfully, we were now traveling roughly parallel with the freeway above us. Then our car, on its own, turned and started back up the Virgin Narrows and came to a stop near the freeway.

Miraculously, our lives had been spared without the slightest injury, and we bowed our heads in prayer to thank our Heavenly Father.

Naturally, the car suffered considerable damage to the undercarriage and rear wheel. However, we received the kind help of a good Samaritan who followed us at a considerable reduction in speed, until we were able to arrive at Mesquite, Nevada for the critical repairs. We then proceeded to Las Vegas, attended the funeral and returned home safely to our family.

The Lord truly watched over and blessed us. How grateful we are now that our lives were extended to enable us to fulfill our larger mission in life.

BY MAREN DROUBAY

The Moonlit Hours

In the moonlit hours, I am awoken again by a deafening cry.

Like clockwork. I walk myself to the medicine cabinet. Then to the sink to warm some rags. The moon glows brightly through the windows of our sleepy home.

My toddler howls loudly, as I drag my tired, feeble body to his bedside.

"His feet are cramping." I think with a sigh. This is a battle we've fought together valiantly, night after waking night for four years now. Yet, to his side I go again.

I stroke his hair.

I administer the medicine, wrap his feet in the warmth of the rags, and begin to rub them gently. My hands have memorized this midnight dance.

"It will get better soon, my son." I whisper in the dark. This task feels heavy, laborsome, monotonous; especially to a nursing mother who will soon rise again to answer the next midnight cry.

Motherhood so often calls in the moonlit hours, doesn't it?

Still, my hands refuse to give up until his feet soften, and his cries fade into the dark.

I can't help but weep as I ponder my ever-deepening exhaustion.

But then, in the stillness, *His* words come clearly to a weary mother's mind:

"Inasmuch as ye have done it unto the least of these, my brethren, ye have done it unto me."

And suddenly, I can clearly see the Savior washing his disciples feet.

His loving hands, performing a gentle dance, like mine.

And so clearly, I can see Him praying and kneeling. Lifting and healing.

Often in the moonlit hours.

Tears of gratitude slip down my cheeks and land on the toes of my son, finally still.

"What an honor." I think- to serve the Savior of the world at midnight, with tired eyes, and weak hands. I know He sees, and I know He is near. I can sense the warmth of *His* hands around mine as I perform my exhausting, sacred and holy moonlit task.

Dear weary Mama, In the bringing of a fussy infant to your chest; or attempting to break a fever. In the comforting, the kissing, the holding, the patting; the burping and shushing and singing and rocking; in the bouncing, the nursing, the endless bottle making:

I gratefully testify to you. You are doing as He did.

He has *unceasingly* come to *me* in the moonlit hours of motherhood.

And He is *unceasingly* beside *you* in your lonely moonlit hours too.

BY AMBER HODGES

Fighting For Me

A few Decembers ago, my youngest son--three years old at the time--fell from our 26-foot, second story window toward our concrete porch.

I was home with him and my middle son. The two of them were up in our loft where the window is located, admiring the first big snowstorm of the winter. That window has a window seat, and Baylor was standing on it with his full body pressed against the screen and window pane.

For reasons still unknown, that window was opened and Baylor went tumbling end over end, right out the window. My middle son came running downstairs screaming, having watched his brother in that freefall, and I tore out the front door to find him on top of a mangled window screen on the ground.

I'll spare the extensive details, but we spent several harrowing hours in the emergency room, running scans and other tests. As his mother, I was in a lot of shock at that time.

There was one specific moment during the MRI,

when the magnitude of what was happening to my family set in a bit. He was terrified of going in the tube for the scan, and was screaming and crying out to me. I was the only person in the room with him as the techs ran the scan just beyond a glass window, and I felt very alone.

I pleaded at that moment for *Him* to send me some-one. I needed someone with me as I watched helplessly, unable to fix the pain or to comfort my baby. At that mo-ment, I distinctly heard the words, *"I'm right here."* and I knew He was aware of us.

Miraculously, Baylor was able to come home with us that day with minor injuries. My story of how *He* came for me actually takes place in the days that followed:

I had never known anxiety or depression before that event, so I wasn't exactly sure what was happening to me as the heavy darkness settled around me in those days. I couldn't seem to convince my mind and heart that we had been immensely blessed and witnessed a miracle, as my son--although unable to walk--was ok after that fall.

Everytime I tried to close my eyes to sleep, I pic-tured his little body tumbling through the air. In the dark-ness, I could hear the thud of his body connecting with the ground. Thoughts of being an inadequate mother whose carelessness had led her son to this experience were on re-peat in my mind. I didn't sleep for days, and spent a lot of time in my dark closet trying to hide from it all, in vain.

During one of my closet visits, I threw up a desperate plea to heaven. I felt so dark, and so alone. Immediately, I had an image come to mind of darkness and light, and they seemed to be pressing against each other. The light was easily overtaking the darkness. The image was quick, but it left a distinct impression that while Satan was fighting really hard to break me, my Savior was fighting just as hard FOR me. The creator of the universe and Messiah of the world, was fighting for ME--a broken young mother, in a small town, hiding in her closet.

His atonement was no longer just about sin and justice in that moment for me, it was about grace. It was about mercy. It was about such individualized love and devotion. I had never understood this facet of Christ's mission until that moment in my closet, when I realized that He came for me specifically.

BY LACEY SWENSON

Dumpster Diving

I'd like to tell you about the first time I "met" Jesus. I was seven years old, living in poverty and experiencing neglect and abuse. I didn't know anything about God or Jesus but my soul knew Him the moment I saw Him.

My mom would frequently go dumpster diving in Salt Lake City, behind the thrift store in the valley, local to us.

One night, she took me with her and told me I could pick one thing. I remember her telling me to be really quiet while we went to find the dumpster. It was tall and white and I had to scramble up it like a monkey to peer inside.

When I finally hoisted my little body up and over to see what treasures were waiting for me, the first thing I saw was *His* eyes.

It was a large sixteen by twenty-inch painting. Instantly I recognized who *He* was, but I had no recollection of ever meeting Him.

I asked my mom "Who is that?"

She responded, "I'm not sure- some guy."

As she dug around and looked, I couldn't take my

eyes off of Him. My little heart fluttered and I felt a longing like I'd never experienced before.

He was wearing a red robe with a white shirt underneath. He had shoulder-length hair with a beard, and the most beautiful and kind face I had ever laid eyes on. I decided that was the treasure I wanted to take home, but she wouldn't let me take it.

I never forgot His face, but I couldn't put my finger on who He was until I went into foster care at ten-years-old.

The first time I walked into a church with my foster family, they had that *exact painting* of Jesus Christ in the foyer. It stopped me dead in my tracks and I knew:

He had always been there; sending me small love notes like the one He sent me that one night in a dumpster.

BY HEATHER G. PREECE

They Need You

In the summer of 2017, I spent every morning in my closet having a panic attack.

After losing three babies to miscarriages in the span of eight months, I had given birth to a healthy baby boy in April. Things should finally be perfect, and I should finally be happy.

Instead, I was immediately taken over by feelings of panic, dread, and worry.

Little things would happen, and I would feel like I couldn't handle it. My older children would fight, and I would instantly cry. My baby would be sleeping for what felt like too long, and I would fear that he died. I had never heard of postpartum anxiety before, but I would later be diagnosed with it and put a name to all the things I was feeling and experiencing. One of the hardest parts of this experience was the accompanying intrusive thoughts.

They are called intrusive for a reason. They are unwanted. They are horrible. They are graphic. They are mean. They come without warning at the lowest point of the day and aren't anything you would wish on your worst enemy. They are disturbing. They are distressing. And they are often repetitive.

My most frequent and repetitive intrusive thought: *"Your kids would be better off without you. You are the worst mom."* This would come to me when I was driving down a winding road and would take all my willpower not to swerve. This would come to me when my kids were fighting, and I would cry in the corner knowing someone else would handle this better.

This would come to me when I was holding my precious newborn as I looked into his perfect eyes and knew that somehow, someway, I would mess this up for him and his life would be miserable because his mom wasn't mentally tough enough to get through this.

I have a background in psychology and counseling, and I knew the importance of social support and getting help. I knew the signs I should be looking for were more than an adjustment period to having a new baby.

I knew that there was help available for me but my intrusive thoughts kept convincing me that I should be able to do this on my own. I was convinced that this was just what my life was going to look like from now on, and that I should just figure out how to handle it.

In the midst of all of this, I was having a particularly hard morning. I came out of my "closet panic attack" and looked at my red, swollen eyes in the mirror. The intrusive thoughts came rolling in one after another. I felt I couldn't take it anymore. The thoughts were persistent, and they had worn me down so much that I no longer felt

I could fight them off. In the middle of these loud, unrelenting thoughts, I felt an inspiration come to my heart.

I heard a quiet reassurance in just three simple words: *they need YOU.*

After months of hearing in my head thoughts of not being good enough, of how weak I was, of my kids being better off without me, my pattern was broken up with this subtle encouragement. I knew it came straight from heaven to my heart.

I think the most important part of this story is that it didn't end there. I wasn't suddenly cured of my intrusive thoughts, but it was a very important first step to keep moving forward. It was a step to realize that what I had been experiencing was, in fact, not normal postpartum issues- and something I needed help to overcome.

I finally told my husband and my social support what I had been experiencing. I made an appointment with my doctor, and he told me about postpartum anxiety – a phrase that was completely foreign to me up until this point.

I started medication which gave me the desire to want to get better. I don't know that I would have ever gained that desire and motivation without it. After that, I took the next step and started therapy. Therapy helped me work through the trauma of my miscarriages, which, in turn, led to healing from a traumatic post-birth experience, hypervigilance over my baby, and crushing anxiety. I began to heal from the outside in. I started to go outside, even for a few minutes, every day and became less anxious about taking my kids out with me. I started to practice joyful movement and focused on nourishing my body and getting sleep.

This wasn't an overnight change for me, but each day I felt myself getting better. When I would have an exceptionally hard day, I would remind myself of the inspiration I received – *that my kids needed me.* Even in my brokenness. Even in my struggles. Even in my feelings of inadequacy. Even with my anxiety. Even with my stress.

They needed me.

I've come to understand this is a universal lesson – They need *you.*

Exactly as you are and exactly who you are. The world needs the person that you are and they need you to be authentically you.

Since that time, I have applied this lesson to all areas of my life and realize that I make better, more genuine connections when I show up as myself because that is what the people around me need.

I am a better school counselor when I listen and respond with my genuine thoughts and feelings versus thinking about what technique is best in this situation or what other people would say and do. That's when I can create a real connection with kids.

I am a better professor when I spend less time trying to fit a mold, and more time sharing what I'm passionate about and connecting with students. I've come to terms with the fact that I will never get reviews that say, "she is brilliant," or "she is the smartest professor in the department," but will consistently get reviews that say, "she is so passionate about the subject,"and "she makes me feel loved." The students in my class need me as I really am, not as the inauthentic version of myself that I sometimes expect myself to be.

I am a better friend when I share my struggles, listen to my friends, and don't try so hard to be perfect or popular. It's easy to put out in the world the parts of our lives that seem flawless or acceptable.

It's more difficult to be honestly genuine, admit that we struggle, and reach out for help. At the core of it all, we need connection. We need each other. We need to feel like someone understands us and our experiences or, at the very least, cares about our experiences. We need to know that someone is willing to meet us where we are at. We need to know that we will still be loved when we mess up because we are going to mess up. We need to know that we will still be loved when we are sad or broken. We need people to laugh with, cry with, celebrate with, and break down with.

This is why real stories matter. This is why I tell my story even though it exposes the most vulnerable parts of my soul. By exposing my soul, I hope it helps someone else to feel okay to share parts of their soul too, and not feel so alone.

Recently my son wrote in his school journal, "my mom loves everyone... She loves to learn and loves to be silly." Before I had kids, I would have said that the ideal image of motherhood I had included having a spotless house, constantly baking, attending PTA meetings, and having kids who could play piano at a concert level, budding artistic abilities, and excelling at sports. And maybe this is what motherhood looks like for you, and that's great if that's who you are!

But who I authentically am, is someone who loves everyone, loves to learn, and loves to be silly. And the fact that my kids can see that and know that's who I really am, means they know they can be *who they really are too* and that is what my kids need.

Because they need me. "They need you" and you are needed too.

BY TISH WHITE

Butterflies

Nearly six years ago I was diagnosed with Lupus and Rheumatoid Arthritis.

Since then, it has been a roller coaster of challenges to find relief from the pain these diseases cause. Countless doctor appointments, blood draws, injections, MRIs, and failed biologics. I do all the things: meditate, yoga, sleep (lots and lots of sleep), eat healthily, pray, and the list goes on. And to no avail, I continue to suffer in pain every single day.

After years of faithful hope, it was like the gas had started to run out and there was nothing left but fumes. I just didn't know how to keep going and stay positive; it felt insurmountable. I had prayed countless times that I could be healed or that we could find a medication that would help. I felt like my prayers went unanswered. I felt insignificant and like God couldn't hear my prayers.

I felt more alone than ever.

At this point, I remember saying one of the most

broken-hearted prayers I have ever said. It went something like this:

"Heavenly Father, I am so broken right now and I feel like you can't hear me. I feel like you don't care. I feel like you have abandoned me. I am in so much pain, and I'm ready for my miracle. But I'm also ready to let everything go and turn it all over to you. I can't carry this anymore. It hurts too much, it's too heavy, so I'm giving it to you. I know that you might not be able to heal me right now or help me find the right medications, but can you please just help me know that I am not alone? God, can you please help me know that you can hear me? I don't know, maybe it's crazy, but can you please just send me some kind of sign? Can you just send me a butterfly or something and then I'll know that you're here with me?"

I have always loved butterflies, because there is so much significance in their process of becoming a butterfly. There is beauty within all of the mundane and ugly stages of their creation.

And the same goes for us.

I nearly forgot about my prayer the next day. I was going through the Swig drive-thru to grab a drink, and the cashier randomly said "I love your butterfly earrings!"

I told her "thank you" and reciprocated the compliment and went on my way, thinking nothing of it. Next, I was on Instagram and clicked on a story, and it was what seemed to be a random video of a beautiful monarch butterfly flying from flower to flower.

It wasn't random, nothing is.

It finally clicked, God was sending me my butterflies- and I started to bawl.

It was then that I heard the Holy Spirit saying to

75

me "God never abandoned you, you just stopped looking for him".

Over the next month, I had some major health challenges. I kept looking- and God continued to send me butterflies! Sometimes it was simple, like a picture in a children's book, and other times it was magical - like thousands of butterflies in a field that we were driving by.

I knew that He was there, mindful of me, and listening.

I've learned that God meets you right in the middle of your brokenness, and sometimes that's in the drive-thru at Swig - or even on Instagram! You just have to have an open heart and be looking for him. And if things feel too heavy, let God take a turn carrying it.

Maybe my miracle won't ever come, but I know that God loves me because he sent me his Son. He has given me a way to return to him someday, pain-free and covered in his love.

I also know that he loves me and hears my prayers because every once in a while on the extra hard days, he still sends me butterflies.

BY SHERRY HOWARD

Broken Pieces

I woke up unexpectedly in the middle of the night.

I sat up in bed and reached onto my night stand, grabbing my notebook and pen, and wrote these words. The words were this:

Heavenly Father shows me through the broken pieces of life that his light comes through.

I have had many moments, experiences, and even seasons in my life where I felt broken. I have had times of grief where my life felt a bit too much to bear.

Those broken pieces at times were even too much for me to carry alone; but the reality is that *His light has always come through every time.*

It radiates a warmth in my heart and my soul that fills me up and helps me and heals me.

I know that I will have more broken pieces in my life. That is part of our mortal existence. These broken pieces, no matter how big or small, build me, shape, mold, and help me grow into the woman Heavenly Father needs me to be- not just for myself, but also to be a light to others.

Embrace our broken pieces. Know that they are necessary to become who we are destined to be. Take your broken pieces and put them together to build your foundation. We are all broken. That's how the light comes in.

May you be a light and a strength for yourself and others. Know that you are never alone.

BY HEIDEE SPENCER

I'm Walking the Halls With You

I was in a rough season. I was in the depths of severe post-partum depression.

Changes, big emotions from the big (and little) people; it had been hard.

The dust started to settle in our lives and I felt like I was somewhat coming out of the fog, but still felt lifeless and disconnected.

I was at church and spending yet another sacrament meeting, pacing the halls with an upset baby. Our ward building had just gotten new artwork throughout the building the week before.

As I paced the halls with my baby in my arms, I tried to show her the new art:

"Look sweetie. Do you see Jesus? Where is Jesus?" I asked her.

Then I thought to myself, "Yeah Jesus, where are you? Haven't really felt you around lately."

As I stared at this picture of Jesus, I heard a voice say: *"I'm here with you. I'm walking the halls with you."*

Then memories popped into my head of the last few months. Things that hadn't seemed divine at the time, I could now see as clear divine love and intervention for me specifically.

Like on a particularly dark day, a friend that lives over an hour away drove to my house to leave my favorite treat on my porch! Or when I couldn't go to the gym anymore, and a kind stranger gave me a treadmill- and when that treadmill was too heavy for me to lift and transport home, family members dropped what they were doing to come help.

My Heavenly Father never forgot me. My Savior never forgot me. They placed incredible people in my path to hold me together, carry me and my family, and share God and Jesus Christ's love for me with me.

Since that moment in the church hallway I remind myself constantly:

"I'm here with you. I'm walking the halls with you."

I'm never alone. I just need to look; His love is there.

BY JORDAN FAIRBOURNE

He Keeps His Scars For Me

At my six week check up with my first child, I was diagnosed with postpartum depression. I really struggled to feel connected to her, and felt like I was failing as a mother.

A month later, I found out I was expecting again. I was so scared. I already had one baby that I didn't feel I could take care of, and now I was supposed to take care of another one?!

This shook up our entire lives. My husband left for school four hours away to get a better job, and I moved in with my parents to help save some money while I was also finishing school.

My second baby was born, and my husband graduated from school in the same week.

We moved to Utah a month later and then COVID-19 happened. I had never felt more isolated in my life. My faith in Christ took the biggest hit. I felt like I couldn't go anywhere to find the answers I wanted.

I continued to work for my faith and found that I had a much stronger testimony than I realized. One day, while reading Isaiah 49, verse 16 really hit me. *Christ keeps his scars for ME.*

He knew me so intimately that He knew what I needed before I ever did!

My second baby was the best thing He could have given me. In that moment of weakness, I didn't think a baby would be anything but a detriment. Instead, she has been the biggest blessing. Her entire existence changed the course of my motherhood, my schooling, my marriage, and my faith.

Because of her, I learned how to fully lean on the Lord and His timing. His plan was greater than anything I could ever imagine and, without her, I might not have learned that lesson so deeply.

He does not forget us. He does not forsake us. He scarred His body for us so that we might have eternal life. We are truly His work and glory.

BY SHELBI BRAUN

Holding My Hand

When I was 10 weeks pregnant with my first baby I was diagnosed with thyroid cancer. When I called my OB's office, I was so nervous and just needed to know what I needed to do.

I was talking to a nurse who informed me that if we were doing radiation, I would need to abort my baby. I hung up and started sobbing. I called my mom and my husband to tell them the news.

I was at work, and instantly dropped to my knees; and I started praying.

After I said *amen*, I felt at peace.

I was still so scared and unsure about what would happen, but I felt like my prayers were heard. I met with the oncologist and my primary doctor and they both agreed that I could wait to have surgery until after I delivered!

I went to my OB with the plan, and he was ecstatic and so apologetic.

I gave birth to a beautiful baby girl who is three-years-old now.

I ended up having surgery to remove half of my thyroid- eleven days after delivering my daughter. Since then, my scans have all been clear and my daughter is happy and healthy!

I know without a doubt that Jesus Christ and Heavenly Father were there, holding my hand during that time.

BY DENAE BRANCH

Even In My Anger

I have experienced a lot of loss in the last few years.

I've lost trust in relationships (betrayal trauma).

I've lost people that I love as they've passed away, and we've lost income and financial stability.

We almost lost our home in a house fire, and I've grieved about the future as I have faced the reality of having kids with special needs.

We've experienced loss of good health - both mental and physical.

I feel like I have lost so much this year.

I was actually pretty angry with God for all of my losses, and didn't really understand His plan for me.

How could this be my plan?

What did I do to deserve this? I've always been so obedient and faithful.

One day, I was in Sunday School when my Bishop started talking about Job.

He said something along the lines of, "Job had so much loss in his life and he was mad at God. He questioned

85

God and His plan for him. Job overcame the world, and in the end, his will was God's will; but Job wasn't a perfect person who was totally okay with the hand dealt to him. He was mad."

That story made me bawl like a baby, right there at church, and then again at home.

I felt understood.

And I felt that God was talking to me through my Bishop. He knew I was mad at Him.

And I knew He still loved me in my anger.

And I think God knew then- and still knows- my heart.

I'm a changed person because of all of my losses. I feel more broken, more jaded, and sometimes, I still feel mad. Maybe, like Job, I will overcome the world.

Right now, I'm in the process of a lot of learning and it's been uncomfortable and hard, but I can't say I've been left alone! For that I am so grateful.

It is because of Jesus that we never have to do it alone.

I've seen so many miracles and God's hand in my life through it all.

He came for me over and over again, even when I was angry.

And if you look for Him, I know He will come for you too.

BY HEATHER ELLIS

Mother the Mothers

I work as a birth and postpartum doula.

I was supporting a mama who was having an incredibly hard and long labor. I felt helpless in trying to ease her pain. It was the middle of the night, so I went into the small, dark waiting room, and got on my knees to pray.

I asked my Heavenly Father and my Heavenly Mother for guidance, to know how to best help and comfort this mama.

I had a distinct thought come to my mind:

"Mother the mothers."

I went back to her room and sat next to her, holding her hand and stroking her forehead.

She began to cry, and told me that she never knew how much she needed that simple, comforting touch. She said it made her feel like her mother was there with her, whom she wished was at the birth.

Miraculously her labor began to speed up! Still hard, but it was over soon, and she had a beautiful baby boy. My heart was filled with gratitude for my Heavenly parents, and for the guidance They gave to me and the love they showed both of us.

Their daughters.

BY KELSI PERRY

Hang in There a Little Longer

After having my baby, I went through the darkest moments in my life.

I was at a point where I was having constant panic attacks for two weeks, and nothing was helping. The suicidal thoughts were overwhelming, and I told my husband that he needed to hide any-and-all weapons in the house for the fear of what I would do.

I was desperate for any sort of relief.

One day, rocking back and forth on my bed sobbing and praying out loud for help, *I felt arms wrap around me from behind, and someone holding my hands in front of me.*

The words, *"I know it's so hard right now, but hang in there a little longer. You are not alone."* and the feeling of overwhelming peace and love filled me.

I feel so strongly that it was my Savior and my grandpa that day.

BY BRANDY SALISBURY

He Will Honor Your Faith

My daughter was diagnosed with epilepsy at eight months old.

She was our first, and it was a scary and anxious time in my life.

From that moment on, my anxiety would increase at every doctor appointment or test.

This went on for years and years. I coped with the anxiety and as long as my husband came with me, I could handle it enough to get through.

Then about two years ago, she needed a three-day stay at Primary Children's Hospital for some testing. Only one parent was allowed to stay.

I was terrified!

My anxiety and fear was intense.

In the weeks leading up to the hospital stay, she had a check-up with her pediatrician, and that night I cried, telling my husband that I was so tired of getting anxious with every doctor appointment and test!

I had prayed for strength, but quite honestly that's as far as it went.

I just figured this was my trial in life.

My husband asked me a question that would alter the rest of my life. He said:

"Have you ever asked Christ to take away your anxiety for the doctor appointments?"

I was shook! I rolled my eyes and thought, "Well, yeah I pray all the time, don't I?"

I sat with that question in my heart until the day of her doctor's visit before the upcoming stay at Primary Children's.

As if on cue, the anxiety rolled into my body as soon as I jumped into the car.

I was so upset.

"Why does this keep happening? I can't be the mom I need to be for my daughter if I, myself, can't hold it together!"

And right away, my husband's words entered my mind:

"Brandy, have you asked Him to take it away?"

I didn't even pull over. I just kept driving, and I prayed- harder and more hopeful than I ever have in my life.

"Heavenly Father, I can't do this anymore. I can't be the mom I need to be at these important appointments with this withering anxiety. Please, please take my anxiety away just long enough to complete these important appointments."

As quickly as my anxiety came, it went away. My heart was flooded with peace and comfort, and my anxiety was gone!

As I finished the rest of my drive with tear-stained cheeks, I thanked my Heavenly Father. I thanked Him for hearing me and seeing me, loving and having patience with me.

My favorite part about this story is that the peace did not just happen at that one doctor's appointment. Peace followed me to every one after that- especially our three-day stay, alone at Primary Children's Hospital- nothing but peace, calm and comfort.

Heavenly Father and my Savior, Jesus Christ showed up for me that day in my car.

They guided my husband to say just the right thing, and they *honored my faith when I humbled myself to ask.*

And they continue to honor that faith *every single day.*

BY MAGGIE WILCOCK

I Can Do Hard Things

My husband and I struggled with infertility for ten years.

We have our three miracles now, thanks to IVF, but it was not an easy path to get to. There were many ups and downs with our journey, but I never questioned why.

It was difficult; there were hard days, and days of tears, but my saying during all of this was,

"Come What May and Love It."

I have seen God's hand in my life when it comes to timing, and knew that He would never break His promise.

I knew if we couldn't have kids in this life, we would in the next life.

During these ten hard years, we were placed in positions that allowed us to help multiple youth in our neighborhood who became "our children" for several years!

We were blessed to have them in our home daily (they all had our garage code), and we were their rides to-and-from places. Our pantry became their place of endless snacks, we got to take them on their senior trips, and we taught a few to drive!

We have had the opportunity to take them through the temple and watch some of them get married. My husband actually got to perform one of the wedding ceremonies during Covid, when Temples weren't open! If we had our three kids right away, we would never have been blessed with these opportunities and we would never have been a part of the lives of these fifteen youth, who taught us so much and helped us to grow as individuals.

God's timing has been so crucial in my life, and there is no denying He knows the plan and what is best for us.

IVF was hard, but I feel so thankful and blessed because of it.

It made me stronger.

I met people who I never would have, and I've been able to help others with their IVF journey.

It's taught me that I can do hard things.

God is always there, even when we don't think he is.

BY STEFANI ANDERSON

His Arms Wrapped Around Me

When I was much younger, I got into a bad marriage.

It was abusive, scary, and I was incredibly lonely. I made the very difficult decision to leave. As a result, I had nothing, and I moved back in with my parents.

The pain, grief, and loneliness that comes with divorce is impeccable.

It felt like there was a giant black hole in my chest. I made myself busy, trying to rebuild and repair that hole. One night, I was laying in bed trying to fall asleep and I couldn't get the ugliest thoughts out of my head.

I was shaming myself into oblivion for not making it work, and blaming myself for all that had happened.

The tears started coming and just wouldn't stop. I began to truly plead with Heavenly Father to just let me sleep. I had never prayed so hard in my life!

I finished my prayer, tears pouring down my face, trying to breathe; and something happened. *I felt my Savior very strongly and I felt His arms wrap around me.*

It was warm, kind, and so tender. Peace flowed

through my soul and I was finally able to catch my breath. I quickly drifted off to sleep.

My life and faith have never been the same since that night.

BY HOLLIE

He Came For Me At Play Group

A year after I had my first baby, I found myself living in a new state away from family. My husband had a new job and was working a lot. I also found myself dealing with the unexpected challenge of Postpartum Anxiety.

I was on medication and I was doing everything I could think of to try to help ease the constant overwhelm and loneliness I felt everyday.

My heart ached to have someone who understood how I felt, or to have mom friends who I could talk to about the challenges of being a new mom. I didn't have any friends that lived nearby, and as my daughter was getting older and more social, I yearned to have other moms to have playdates with.

I wanted to put myself out there and make friends, not just for me, but for my daughter too yet my anxiety held me back.

I have never been good at making friends. I have only ever needed a few good friends to surround myself with, but living in a new place while learning how to be a mom made it even more difficult for me to navigate how to make friends.

During the summer, young moms in our area would gather together once a week at different parks to have a big play date with all the kids, and the moms were able to connect with one another.

I had known about this for a while, and I had felt prompted to go.

I knew it was the perfect opportunity for me to meet other moms, and possibly form a friendship in a more casual setting! It was the type of gathering that everyone was invited to.

When they sent around an announcement with the time and place of the playdate every week, it even said, "All are welcome!" on it.

Yet for some reason I could never get myself to go. It felt like I hadn't been personally invited, so it would be weird for me to show up!

The other moms had been doing it together for so long, so I felt like I would be the odd one out!

The time would come each week for the playdate, and I would sit at home and feel so guilty because I knew I was supposed to go. I knew it would help me.

But I could not get myself to go.

This went on for months that summer. And I never went to a single one!

I eventually stopped paying any attention to the playdate reminders, because I knew I would never go; but I couldn't let go of the feeling that I needed to find other moms to surround myself with and to help support me through the struggles I was having.

One day towards the end of the summer, I had been struggling more than normal. I was feeling very lonely. I was doing all the things I knew I needed to do when I started to struggle, and one of those things was running.

Running always helped me to clear my mind, and the physical exercise would bring me much needed endorphins.

As I was getting myself and my daughter ready for our run, I sat down and I said a very short prayer.

It was nothing grand.

All I said was, "I'm struggling really bad. Please help this run to be what I need it to be."

And then we were off.

After a few miles, my daughter was getting restless in the stroller, so we stopped at a park further away from our home that we had not been to before. One of her favorite things after patiently sitting in the stroller, was to get out and play at the park! I was feeling better from the run, but I still had an empty feeling inside.

After playing for a while, I was about to pick her up and head home, but the thought came to me, saying, *"Just a little longer!"*

So we stayed a little longer.

Pretty soon, a car pulled up and I recognized the woman who got out as another mom in our neighborhood! I had talked to her very little before, but we started to talk while the kids played. The emptiness inside me was beginning to fill with gratitude for the chance to connect with another mom.

I remember thinking, "This is why I was supposed to stay a little longer, so that I could talk with her."

I was feeling like my prayer had been answered, when another car pulled up and pretty soon another! It took me a moment to realize what was happening.

This was the weekly group play date at the park.

This was the play group that I had been told to go to so many times and I ignored it!

The play group I had never gone to.

So He brought them to me.

I remember talking with all the moms at the park and fighting back tears, because they all thought I was just there for the playgroup! They had no idea I had been waiting for them.

Waiting all summer for them.

He had brought them to me because I couldn't do it myself.

That day in a park, still sweaty from my run, He came to me through them.

BY MEGAN MURRAY

The Miracle of Unanswered Prayers

You know those stories where you were praying for a miracle, and that miracle happened?

They're the ones you always hear at church or on the news.

They're the ones that people tell as a way to say: "If you have enough faith, it'll happen."

Mine isn't one of those stories.

Mine is actually one where the miracle we prayed so hard for never happened.

These are the types of stories you don't hear, but so many need to hear. Especially when they feel they must not have the faith they thought they did, because their miracle didn't happen.

In 2016, we found out we were pregnant with our first child.

Like so many others, we were so excited to have a baby and the adventures that would follow! We thought of the first time they would smile or when they would take their first steps.

The nine months were filled with excitement and nervousness.

Little did we know we weren't going to get the experience we hoped for.

Ramie was born, and everything was seemingly fine. He was a month old when I noticed his first seizure. I can vividly remember it happening.

My husband and I were getting ready to go out to the grocery store. My mother-in-law was going to watch Ramie for us. I was sitting on the couch holding him before we left, and he did some really strange movements. I remember mentioning to everyone that it seemed off. I didn't think much of it after, but the next day, the seizures hit:

One, after one, after one- the seizures kept coming.

After talking to an on-call pediatrician, we took him to the ER.

After running as many tests as they could at the local hospital, they took us by ambulance to the children's hospital. It was test after test. It was confirmed he was having seizures, but they were hopeful this would be a case where he would grow out of them.

Ramie was sent home on seizure meds, and we were told to make a follow-up appointment.

If you haven't figured it out by now, our story wasn't that simple.

Ramie's seizures wouldn't stop. The neurologists

weren't easy to get a hold of, and there would be hours when he would just seize and I had no idea what to do. I had to just wait until they called us back. After not getting enough help for a couple of weeks we decided we needed to take Ramie back into the hospital. We got a new neurologist and she helped us to find answers. It wasn't until he was four or five months old that we would get genetic results back that told us that he had a genetic mutation.

KCNT1- which caused a hard-to-treat, medication-resistant, terminal epilepsy disorder.

These aren't the things you would think you would have to deal with as a first-time parent. Yet here we were. *I would outlive my child.* How do you come to terms with that?

How could this be the life my child was dealt?

Ramie's life was filled with hospital visits, doctor visits, medical equipment, and many more physical challenges. Before we found out it was genetic, we prayed and prayed that it would be something he would outgrow.

He would get priesthood blessing after priesthood blessing- all falling on seemingly deaf ears. *Where was our miracle?* We were faithful, church-going members.

My husband and I both served missions, we were active, and we had church callings! We were doing everything we were told we should be doing, and our faith was there. We were told story after story of these medical miracles. All the church talks we could find were ones where these people had so much faith and "Look at these miracles that happened!"

It started causing a lot of doubt and a lot of resentment toward Heavenly Father.

My faith wasn't strong enough to save my child.

My faith started to crumble.

It seemed like five years of prayers going unanswered - or even being answered in the exact opposite way.

I remember laying next to Ramie one day in the pediatric ICU because of a cold, and just begging Heavenly Father to help heal him.

He struggled with some breathing issues and whenever he got sick it exacerbated it.

There would be nights sitting in a rocking chair, holding him more upright, because he could breathe better that way. I would just sit there in the dark and cry. I felt so alone.

I felt like Heavenly Father had left us. Had left Ramie.

It was five years of my faith taking hit after hit. It wasn't all bad. Ramie brought a spirit into our home that I will forever feel the void of. He was our earthly angel. I learned more from him than anyone else. He gave us laughter and love. He loved life despite its challenges. His smile was heaven. He had the best personality. Holding him could make you feel so loved.

We went on to grow our family through it all. My husband and I got genetic testing done and it showed that we weren't carriers of the gene mutation. We were told it was an almost zero percent chance we would have another baby with the same genetic mutation.

We had our second boy who is neurotypical. No seizure disorder.

Then we went on to have a third boy.

He was a couple of days old when the seizures started.

We had put Ramie on hospice a couple of months before Rylan was born and then to have a second child with seizures, I was *broken*.

How was this happening again?

We took Rylan in, and were told it would shock everyone if it came back the same thing as Ramie. A couple of days later the phone call came. It was the same thing, most likely caused by something called gonadal mosaicism. My world was shattered. The little hope I had that maybe it wasn't, felt like such a stupid thing for me to have felt.

"Of course, Heavenly Father would let it happen again."

If our first miracle didn't happen, how silly was I to think he would give me this one? It was a lot to try and digest.

Our bishop at the time, came over to talk with my husband and me. This would be one of the conversations that would help start changing it all.

I could tangibly feel Heavenly Father being there for me.

I can't thank that bishop enough for helping me to start back toward gaining the faith I had lost.

We were talking about how both my husband and I were struggling. That we felt abandoned. How we did everything we were told to do and it wasn't enough. Heavenly Father wasn't listening.

He sat back and told us how sorry he was for our situation. How he didn't know what to say to help us feel better. He then told us that we weren't bad people for feeling what we were feeling! That Heavenly Father didn't fault us for it!

Not once in our five years after having Ramie, did anyone ever tell us that.

All we would hear is to "just keep going, just keep having faith."

Those were meant to be comforting words, but they weren't! However, that bishop, not knowing what to say, said the thing I needed to hear the most.

I wasn't a bad person. No one could expect us to feel differently. It was okay to be where we were.

Heavenly Father did love us, even if we couldn't feel it.

Jesus would be there to meet us where we were.

Ramie passed away a few short months later after this sit-down.

The weekend of Ramie's passing is a beautiful testament to the Savior meeting us where we were. It was filled with tender mercies and sacred experiences.

In Ramie's passing, he gave me the gift of finding Heavenly Father and Jesus Christ.

That's not to say his passing hasn't been hard. It's been an incredibly rough year without him. It has brought other challenges, but this time I feel like I'm not alone. I've had time to reflect on our time with Ramie.

Although our miracle never came to be and Ramie wasn't healed- our miracle turned out to be *five painstakingly beautiful years with a little boy that taught us so much about life.*

Our miracle was Ramie coming and showing us a whole new world we wouldn't have known!

Our miracle is having knowledge, and being able to use that to take care of Rylan.

Ramie paved the way for his little brother.

The road to building my faith hasn't been easy. I still struggle. I'm still working on my relationship with Heavenly Father and Jesus Christ.

I will forever cherish those moments during Ramie's passing when God was in the details. I couldn't have asked for a better end to his life. As I now have to take another journey with epilepsy with Rylan, I have felt better equipped spiritually.

Times get tough, but God is there.

I hope that by sharing my story it can be one that shows that not all miracles happen; at least not in the way we may have wanted. It doesn't mean you are a bad person or that your faith isn't strong enough. *It is.*

God has a miracle for you. He did it for me. It just came in the form of five beautiful years with an earthly angel.

BY SAMMY BASSETT

Rainbows

August of 2022 was one of the hardest months of my life.

It came with so much heartache, but also so many tender mercies from my Savior.

At the end of July, I found out that I was pregnant and was so excited, but I could tell something was off. We began checking my hormone levels- and then I started bleeding.

I was so scared that I was losing my baby, but I tried to hold out hope that all would be well. We continued checking hormone levels and things were looking like they might be okay.

During this same time, my Papa P, one of my very favorite people in the world, was admitted to the hospital. He had been in and out of the hospital multiple times in the prior months and had always come back home.

During that time that he had been sick I had always been by his side. I visited him often and used my nursing knowledge to be his advocate at all of his doctors appointments.

This time, he had an antibiotic-resistant infection

and I was scared to go visit while I was fighting so hard to keep my baby. I called him and spoke to him over the phone and his doctors called me each day to give me an update and answer my questions.

Then one day I got my hormone levels back, and they had dropped.

I called my doctor's office and the nurse told me that I had miscarried, and that the levels would not come back up. I was devastated.

To cheer me up and help the family heal, my husband loaded us up and took us to Disneyland (which happens to be my very favorite place!)

I was so excited to go, and also nervous to leave while Papa was sick.

Everyone told me that I needed to take care of myself first and so I went.

On the drive to California, I received a call from Papa's physician. She did not have good news for me. The infection had spread to his heart, and he was now in a complete heart block.

The upper chambers and lower chambers of his heart were not communicating. They put him on a pacemaker, and there would be a meeting with a surgeon in the morning to discuss the options.

My heart was so heavy. I had lost my baby and now I was going to lose my Papa.

That night we went to some of my favorite places in Anaheim, and I did my best to soak it all up and enjoy every second.

The next morning, I received a call from the surgeon

to discuss the options before the family meeting that would take place. In my heart I knew which option Papa was going to choose, but I didn't want to believe it. I tried listening in to the family meeting while we ate lunch at Disneyland, but I couldn't hear much.

A little bit later my mom called and told me that Papa wanted to go. He did not want to do the surgery. He just wanted to be done.

We knew we needed to get home as soon as possible so that we could say goodbye. I kept soaking up as much fun as I could while searching for flights back home while standing in line. We finally decided that we would just drive home through the night. We went on one more ride before leaving the park. It was 'Soarin' Over the World'.

I will never forget the moment when I explained to my seven-year-old that we had to leave Disneyland early and skip the beach so that we could go home and say goodbye to Papa.

We both sobbed in the line, and everyone gave us funny looks, but I didn't mind.

I called Papa on the way home and told him that I was so sorry for not having been there to visit him, and told him that we were coming back to see him.

It was the last fully lucid conversation I had with him.

On the way home from California, we were able to stop in Vegas and pick up my sister who flew in from Phoenix. We even experienced some car trouble, but we made it home safely.

I wanted to fall apart, but *I could feel my Savior with me every step of the way giving me strength.*

That morning we went to the hospital and the entire family was able to be in the room as we took Papa off the pacemaker, took pictures with him, gave him a blessing, and spent time as a family.

I held his hand til late into the night, and finally went home.

Two days later I was getting ready to go up and see him when my mom called and said that he had just passed. The whole family went up and we gave him one last hug and walked through the halls while they played 'Taps' and gave him a veterans ceremony on his way out of the hospital.

The charge nurse that was working that night was a nurse that I knew from my time working at that hospital! What a relief it was to have a familiar face come in to care for him after his passing.

His funeral was beautiful, and I was able to speak about our favorite memories and how much he meant to me. Before he passed Mama had made him promise that he would send her a sign when he was up in Heaven, so that she would know that he was happy.

The night after the funeral, *family members in three different states saw rainbows appear in the sky at the same time.* We knew this was our sign that he was happy and okay up there.

A week after the funeral, I started having severe cramping on my right side.

At first it went away with some Advil, but soon it wouldn't go away at all.

I said a prayer and asked Heavenly Father if I should

go to the ER, and immediately felt at peace knowing that I needed to go in.

We did some blood work and an ultrasound and found out that I actually had not miscarried. I was still pregnant with an ectopic pregnancy and my tube had ruptured. I was bleeding internally and would be whisked away for emergency surgery.

My husband gave me a blessing and I was taken into the OR. The last thing I remember before falling asleep was *Papa P holding my hand.*

When I woke up in the recovery room he said, "You did good, Miss Mary." and then he left.

I remember telling my husband that I just didn't understand why I had to lose so much all at once. He told me that it was a blessing that my surgery was after Papa's funeral so that I did not have to miss out on anything. He also reminded me that this way, Papa was able to be there for me in a way that would not have been possible if he were still alive!

My heart felt so broken, but I felt so much love from my Heavenly Father.

He was there with me every step of the way and blessed me in numerous ways.

He gave me a wonderful day at my favorite place to help ease the pain of my losses and He sent us rainbows so that we would know Papa was okay. He gave me that last phone call and He helped me get home safely so I could hug Papa and tell him how much he meant to me. He sent me a nurse I knew to give me a hug and take such good care of Papa after his passing and He sent my Papa to comfort me during my surgery. He sent me so many angels that brought dinners and words of comfort and sweet gifts.

We will never be immune to heartache or grief.

The storms of life will come, but if we will just look up, we will always see rainbows. During those hard times we will always be able to find good, to find beauty.

Heavenly Father will come to us and give us peace and comfort. He knows you, He knows your heart, and He is there for you every single step of the way.

No matter how hard life gets he will always be there *if you just take a moment to look for Him.*

BY CARLIE PETERSON

The Light of Christ Shines Through

All my life, I always wanted to be a mom.

I think I played with dolls till I was around eleven years old!

I babysat every chance I could. I loved kids.

My husband and I got married in 2015, and shortly after, I was "baby hungry".

We bought a dog to try and feed that desire, but it didn't last long. After the April 2016 general conference we felt the prompting to start our family.

We tried, and tried, and tried. I broke inside.

Not being able to get pregnant caused me to take a huge part of who I was and what I believed in all my life- my testimony and my faith- and I buried it.

I started to slip away from Christ. It was his fault.

He did this. He knew that all I wanted to be was a mother, and He took that away.

I was so angry. I hid from my family, friends and even my husband.

The hurt was so deep.

My husband and I had finally decided to run all the tests on each of us and start the process of fertility treatments. The bills got expensive, only to be told, kids were probably not in the cards for us.

Again, I broke.

In December of 2016, I had an ultrasound to see if we could tell when I might be ovulating, and it showed nothing. It was no help.

We went out of town for New Years, and when we got back, I had lost all faith.

I told my husband we were done trying.

I couldn't emotionally do it anymore.

On January 4, 2017, I slipped down our apartment stairs and fractured a few ribs, bruised the rest, and hurt my back. I had x-Rays to diagnose that.

On January 22, 2017 my husband told me we needed to attend our stake conference.

I was so upset. I didn't want to go sit through a few-hour church meeting, being told how, "We need to be better saints and follow and trust in the Lord."

I had done that my entire life and he repaid me by making it not possible to have a family! But of course, I went.

The entire stake conference, the talks all spoke deeply to me. (I didn't admit it). Yet each and every one was directed right at me.

Our Stake President got up to close the meeting, and he spoke on our faith during trials.

The whole time he spoke, I kept getting a "feeling" that I needed to go home and take the last pregnancy test that was under the bathroom sink- just to get "rid" of it.

I ignored it, and went home and took a nap. I slept for four hours!

When I woke up, I was so sick, I ran to the bathroom and threw up.

Again, I got the "feeling" to take the pregnancy test.

I pulled it out reluctantly and peed on the stick.

Within seconds I had a positive test in my hands.

I. Was. Shocked. I didn't believe what I was seeing. I came out of the bathroom sobbing.

My sweet husband came up to me and wrapped his arms around me. I told him the news.

I told him we needed to go to Walmart and buy every single brand of pregnancy tests and I needed to take every single one of them to verify!

So away we went. $67 later, at least ten pregnancy tests that had been peed-on sat in front of us. Eleven positive tests.

Monday morning, I called our doctor. He was so shocked and told me to come in for an ultrasound to verify. He sat there for a brief minute, then turned and looked at my husband and I, and said, "I have a question. Do you believe in miracles?"

We both answered yes.

He then asked, "I am not sure what faith you are, but I believe this baby is a miracle. I say this because you are 8 1/2 weeks pregnant."

Like I said above, I had an ultrasound less than three weeks prior, and x-rays less than two weeks prior- that didn't show a thing. Nothing. But I was almost nine weeks pregnant.

How?! By a miracle.

Christ taught me a valuable lesson.

He has blessed us with two beautiful girls, who call me mom.

We are once again struggling to grow our family. We have been struggling for a year and a half. I've now had five miscarriages.

I have gone through the anger, the emotional strain of feeling like it's my fault, and so much more.

Yet the light of Christ still shines bright for me.

I trust him, I know He knows the "big picture", and that He knows me.

Does it mean our trials are any easier? Absolutely not.

But we know first-hand- *how losing the light of Christ made past trials so much harder and darker.*

I personally know that I never walk alone.

There are still times I feel alone, but I have learned to ask where He is and why I don't feel him. I'm so grateful for my trials; they are good reminders of where my faith and trust is, and how strong it truly is.

BY ANONYMOUS

Reaching and Rescuing

The story starts when we moved states and were not by family anymore.

We had two boys, and had a brand new baby shortly after moving. Three months after that, my marriage completely fell apart due to mental illness. On the outside, I looked like I had things together, but on the inside I was a total mess. My heart was broken, devastated, confused, yet hopeful and faith-filled.

I would get all three kids and myself ready for church and go, because I knew that was where I needed to be. There were days my oldest didn't have socks or shoes on at church because it wasn't worth the battle!

We were there.

Throughout the next two months, God rescued me through earthly angels.

I had a ministering sister that would randomly come over and drop off meals.

I had another neighbor randomly bring me a loaf of bread one day.

I had neighbors watch my kids last minute so I could go to counseling appointments and the temple.

I was overwhelmed with the task of moving back to my home state alone with my kids, but knew it must be done. I would kneel down at night and cry in prayer with exhaustion, gratitude and faith- pleading for courage, and much much more.

Then, with all the strength and help from my Savior, I would get up, kick into survival mode, and keep going.

A few days before I was supposed to fly back home, my parents and brother called me.

They booked flights and rented a moving truck and were on their way to help me.

I knew without a doubt that God sees me.

He hears my pleading heart and prayers, and *He is active in reaching and rescuing when we seek Him.*

BY KARLI CLEAVER

He Came In the Forgiving

It was moments before we'd be face to face with someone I had been trying to forgive for over *THREE YEARS*. My husband hugged me and reassured me that it would be a good day. As soon as he left the room, I hit my knees and pleaded with my Father in Heaven. I said something along the lines of, "Please let my thoughts be your thoughts. Let my words be your words. Let everything I do today be motivated by love for my husband and others we love at this gathering. Let me feel the love of your Son in me today."

From the moment we arrived I was intentional about smiling, talking to people, and helping out, while also kind of avoiding direct interaction with 'said someone'. But I felt that nervous anticipation, wondering if I'd receive the help I had asked for, or leave feeling similar conflicting emotions of anger and desperation…just hoping for the peace I know real forgiveness can bring.

A bit later—when this person was sitting alone—something (ahem: the spirit) propelled my body over to sit down beside them. I asked a question about an experience they'd had and spent thirty minutes, listening to and laughing at their story.

During this time, I was FILLED with love for this person. Almost overwhelmingly so! Since that day, I've come to realize that one of the sweetest gifts from the Lord was that I was able to recognize what was happening in real time, AS it was happening. I had ZERO feelings of animosity, anger, bitterness, or hurt. No negativity could cross the barrier created by love. I was even able to vocally express love and be vulnerable.

Immediately upon leaving, the adversary came in full-force, trying to convince me to question my choices to break the ice, to be vulnerable, and to let love in. Just as quickly, the spirit filled my heart and reassured me that I had been vulnerable and open and loving because that is who I am. To have handled the experience any differently would have been hiding Him.

Elder Jeffrey R. Holland (referring to Moses' terrifying encounter with Satan after his heavenly vision with the Father) said, "Like Moses in that vision, there may come, after the fact, some competing doubts and confusion, but it will pale when you measure it against the real thing. Remember the real thing. Remember how urgently you have needed help in earlier times and you got it."

I felt the Savior's love flowing through me as if He were sitting alongside me, encouraging me to let go of the anger and hurt.

I know He was sitting beside me. I could not deny it. It was real.

It's been four months, and even if I tried, I could

not summon anything but an increase of love for this person. The Lord is patient in waiting. He waited til I asked—with a sincere desire to let Him lead the narrative of this story—and until the timing was right, and then He met me where I was and did the heavy lifting so I could just feel the love.

I've often thought that by forgiving someone (especially when it doesn't seem like they care much either way), we are giving them a free pass…a "get out of jail free" card… Like they're getting away with something. But what I learned from my Savior that day is He has already taken it. If we give it to Him (after He's literally already felt it and paid for it), He increases our peace beyond our understanding and takes all the weight we carried as well.

He's already done it, but the responsibility to truly give it up to Him is ours. He won't force our hand. He will love us til we are ready to trust Him with our hard.

Jesus came for me that day. He showed up (spoiler: He always does).

He filled my brokenness with His love far and above what I could have asked or expected with my finite understanding.

I'm forever grateful.

BY KENNEDY WADSWORTH

When Nobody Else Is There

I was a happy first-time mom of a little girl.

She came to us so easily, and we were excited to give her a sibling. Maybe a little sister?! That would be my dream come true. The months went by and I wasn't getting pregnant. I felt so much frustration and heartache; jealousy and drive to do everything just perfect and fix "that one thing" that would be the key to getting pregnant.

I had my first fertility test on Valentines Day and laid there, wondering,

"What am I doing here? Why is everyone else having their second child and I'm here? Why is God taking my children away from me?!"

I held so much anger and blocked Him out.

After a year of trying, fertility testing, and using medication- I got pregnant!

Our miracle was here, and my depression lifted. I experienced a lot of anxiety about our baby but each ultrasound and heartbeat sounded great.

My children were farther apart than planned, but it wasn't too big of a gap. My daughter enjoyed giving me "check-ups" with her pretend stethoscope.

At my sixteen-week check-up, I laid on the table and the doctor couldn't find the baby's heartbeat. He brought in multiple ultrasounds- but it was gone. It was the worst moment of my life.

Though I was alone physically when I was in that room, I remember feeling the presence of Christ. I felt Him there with me through the pain and I'm glad that I wasn't alone.

We learned that we had lost a healthy baby girl for an unknown reason. We had a longer journey ahead to getting our second child here.

My miscarriage broke my heart wide-open to be filled with more compassion and empathy for others, and allowed me to find more joy in the mundane moments when I had my son.

I believe Christ was there for me in that room when no one else could be.

BY REBECCA BECKER

You're Doing A Lot of Things Right!

A few years ago I was struggling with my son. He was probably about twelve at the time, and he was struggling with anxiety and depression and had many big emotions.

I felt stretched and worn, and completely exhausted from the things I was doing to try to help him.

I didn't know what to do or how to handle things most of the time, and I felt like a failure as a parent.

One day, I was at the end of my rope and I knelt down to pray. I poured my heart out to my Heavenly Father, explaining all the things I was doing wrong as a mother, making a long list in my mind.

As I knelt there at the side of my bed, the thought came, *"But you're doing a lot of things right!"* and peace came to my soul. I know it was comfort coming from my Savior who meets me where I'm at. It was a seemingly small thing, but it was big to me, and in that moment I was given the peace and reassurance I needed.

I have often thought of that phrase, *"But you are doing a lot of things right!"* as I make my way through this crazy

125

life, and it reminds me of the grace the Savior gives us and the grace I need to give myself.

We don't have to have big, profound experiences to see the Savior in our lives.

He comes to us time and time again through the everyday things we experience, no matter how mundane or insignificant they seem. He sees the good in us and the efforts we are making! His comforting power gives us the strength to get up and try again.

BY JENESSA KRAMER

Little Details

It was Sunday, and five days before, I had just had my third miscarriage in the second trimester (my fifth miscarriage overall). My D&C was scheduled for Tuesday, and I really didn't want to go to church.

We lived in a small branch where we knew everybody and I wasn't ready to face all of them yet, but I really felt like I needed to go. And in my head, I merely THOUGHT (not even a prayer), "I would love to sing 'I Believe in Christ' today."

It's my favorite hymn.

It came on our playlist the day we brought my little boy home from the hospital. He was our rainbow baby after our twenty-week stillbirth, and the lyrics *"While I strive through grief and pain, His voice is heard ye shall obtain"* hit me so hard.

The fourth verse is my favorite, and has gotten me through so much. So I wanted to sing the song, and I walked into our chapel, sat down, and began to sob when I saw the number 134 up on the song board.

He hears my thoughts, He knows where I am, He knows what I'm going through, and He cares about the *little details.*

"I believe in Christ, so come what may," because I know He's holding me, especially in my lowest moments.

BY ANONYMOUS

Even When We Don't See Him

Last April, I received a message from a number I didn't recognize.

As I read it, I saw that it was from my Stake President, and that he wanted to meet with me. The terrifying thought crossed my mind that Stake Conference was less than two weeks away. So naturally, I panicked for the next five hours until our meeting.

Sure enough, my gut was right. After he asked me to speak, I quickly told him how under-qualified I was to be speaking. I'm not kidding. I probably shouldn't admit this, but I was raised in a family that considered Stake Conference a Sunday where we got to stay at home from Church; so up until this day, I had never been to a Stake Conference, let alone spoken at one!

Then he told me what he wanted me to speak about.

I grew even more nervous.

More doubts raced through my mind. He asked me

to share *my story.* He told me to be vulnerable, and that even if my story only touches one person, that was why he felt the need for me to speak. So I pushed the feelings of inadequacies away and trusted in his guidance that that would be the case. Here is my story that I told that day:

I was raised in Northern California in a family that was active in the church. My mother was a convert to the church in her late teens, and my dad was raised in the church, served a mission in St. Louis, Missouri, and served in the Bishopric.

After relocating to Utah for my Dad's job, our family (as many often do), ran into struggles. My older sister went down a hard path that eventually led to her involvement in drugs and tragically- that's still the case today.

While my father wasn't perfect, I remember him trying to hold our family together in so many ways. I can remember seeing him read his scriptures, going to church, suggesting we have family prayers. I remember him going to the temple where he served every Tuesday night.

Then suddenly on New Years Day, 2003, our family took a direct hit.

This moment in time essentially took us down and changed the trajectory of our lives forever. My father passed away unexpectedly at 47 years old, due to pneumonia.

I was seventeen at the time.

I'll spare you the details of the heartbreaking years that followed, but in short, my family fell apart- just when we needed to pull together. When we needed to learn to lean on the Lord.

We crumbled.

My mom stopped going to church, my younger brother later went down the same path as my sister, and in what seemed like seconds, everything changed. My family, as I knew it, was torn apart. There were no more family dinners, holidays, or birthday celebrations.

There was no more home to go back to.

While I, too, became inactive in the church throughout this time, it wasn't for any reason but pure convenience. The longer I didn't go to church, the easier it became. You tend to not think about it and just go with the motions of life.

If anyone would ask, I would say I still had faith in the gospel and the atonement, but it was marginal at best.

I would occasionally pull out my patriarchal blessing and read it, thinking about how different my life had turned out from what was written on that paper. I ignored any and all promptings and feelings I had to make any changes.

Fast forward twelve years later: I found myself wondering how I was going to keep putting one foot in front of the other. My family members had continued down their paths and it had been years since everyone had gone their separate ways.

I felt utterly alone.

I remember forcing myself on my knees one February evening, while out feeding my horse and sitting there, not even knowing what to say or where to begin.

I believed and felt it so deep in my soul that I had gone too far down this path of being inactive, and I was not in a position to even be kneeling there!

Suddenly, sitting on the dirt and surrounded by bales of hay, *I felt this warm feeling come over me.*

For the first time in a very long time, I felt the spirit.

I questioned it at first, but it grew stronger as my tears grew heavier.

Genesis 28:16 reads: *"Surely the Lord is in this place; and I knew it not."*

He had been there all along and I just wasn't listening. I wasn't looking. He had been waiting.

A few days later, I received a call from a friend who said they felt like they needed to call me and invite me to go to church with them tomorrow. I quickly said no, but then proceeded to not sleep at all that night.

That Sunday I went back to church for the first time in over twelve years.

I drove an hour into Salt Lake City, and went to that random ward with my friend. It took every ounce of courage in me to walk in those doors. All through the sacrament, I remember feeling so calm and thinking, "This is just what I need."

As soon as the closing hymn started, I ran back to my car. I had many tears and emotions on the drive home that day. All I knew was that I needed to keep going.

Each Sunday, I would make that drive, sneak into the back, just as sacrament was starting, and leave during the closing prayer or song.

That hour was what got me through to the next week.

A few weeks after I started going back to church, I found a lump that was concerning to my doctor.

While speaking with a dear friend of mine, she told

me her father would give me a priesthood blessing- my first priesthood blessing in so long.

Just as my friend's father started my blessing he paused, and after a few moments tearfully said, "Heavenly Father wants you to know that you are on the right path. Keep going and have faith."

He told me that I need to learn to lean on my friends as they would become my family.

I knew that night that I needed to keep my eyes on the temple, and stay focused on that.

One day as I was making my escape after sacrament, the Bishop came racing after me in the parking lot. He quite literally must have left during the closing hymn in order to catch me! It was during those few moments of conversation, that I realized I was right where I needed to be.

He welcomed me into that ward with open arms and helped me work toward achieving my goal. I remember meeting with him many times.

During one of our visits, he told me that I reminded him of his mother, who single handedly led his family down the beautiful path of the gospel of our Savior Jesus Christ and eternal families. He told me that I, too, could set an example for my future prosperity.

That thought had never occurred to me.

I could change the pattern and benefit future generations.

The next year on February 13th, 2016 I went through the Jordan River Temple! I had so many wonderful people there supporting me that night.

Inside the temple and out. None of which were my family.

However, the Jordan River temple was where my father served every Tuesday night and because of our great plan of happiness, the veil was thin for me.

I'll always remember sitting there afterwards with a close friend (whom I had just met the year prior, and I was honored to have her as my escort). We were talking about families, and she told me that she could just imagine my kids watching me at that moment- knowing that I had experienced my struggles and hardships alone, so that when it would be their turn on earth, they wouldn't have to go alone. *I would be right beside them.*

It's funny, looking back, how I can see the hand of God in some many of the small and big details of that time.

From that moment out in the field.

To the call to invite me to church.

My friend's father giving me that blessing.

Placement in a ward where the bishop would run after me in the parking lot.

The location of the house I purchased, which then led me to a wonderful friend who ended up being my temple escort on that special day.

My friends who have become like family to me.

In meeting my wonderful husband one random day while mountain biking, when I wasn't supposed to be.

In my husband's dear family welcoming me and loving me- filling a void that sometimes feels so deep.

In the blessing of our two wild special little boys- one of which is the spitting image of my Dad- it's almost scary!

He was in the details. Just because we don't see him, doesn't mean he isn't there.

Fast forward to this last December, we woke up one Friday to a beautiful snowy morning. (We got married in the mountains in the snow, we snowmobile, and we love the snow!)

That snowy morning, we walked into the Brigham City Temple and were sealed as a family for all time and eternity. It was a moment I'll cherish forever.

From listening to the inspired sealer speak to us, to the things he said that my heart needed to hear. From kneeling across from my husband and seeing him start to cry, to watching our little boys come in the room and look all around, bewildered.

I'll remember looking around at the faces of the people who came to support us, knowing that it's because of our Savior Jesus Christ's healing atonement that we had that moment.

The atonement works in my life- just as I know it does for each of our family and friends that were there that special day- just as it does for each and every one of you.

In a 2014 General Conference Talk Elder David A Bednar said, *"There is no physical pain, no spiritual wound, no anguish of the soul or heartache, no infirmity or weakness you or I ever confront in mortality that the Savior did not experience first. In a moment of weakness we may cry out, "No one knows what it's like. No one understands. But the Son of God Perfectly knows and under-stands, for he has felt and borne our individual burdens.*

And because of His infinite and eternal sacrifice, he has per-fect empathy and can extend to us his arm of mercy. He can reach out, touch, succor, heal and strengthen us to be more than we could ever be and help us to do that which we could never do relying only upon our own power. Indeed, His yoke is easy and his burden is light."

I bear my testimony that I know in my heart that the gospel of Jesus Christ is true and that we have a prophet and leaders who are here to guide and direct us today.

I believe in the healing powers of the atonement, and in eternal families.

I believe I'll see my dad again one day, and I know that he still plays a role in my world.

I know that the covenants we make in the temple are so important, and something to not take lightly despite what the world would have us think.

I know that our Savior lives- and when we fall short- He is there to lift us up.

Earthly Angels

God comes for me. He comes in the form of earthly angels at my door, a text or phone call, a sunrise or sunset that speaks to my soul reminding me of His power and His love.

He comes in the pure beauty of the snow, or the sunbeams on my face.

I know he exists with the daily miracles He provides if I just look for His hand!

When I was in my late twenties, I received some heart-wrenching news.

I'll never forget the horrid moment and pure helplessness I felt. In that very moment when I was too weak to stand, hearing the news, He knew what I needed: A stranger- an earthly angel- that showed up and wrapped her arms around me in His place.

The veil has never been so thin in my life, and I have no doubt He came for me in my moment of weakness. He provided comfort during unimaginable pain, He held my heart when it was too painful. I know without a doubt He will come for you too! I love my Savior and the love He provides to all his children.

BY HAILEY REYNOLDS

An Angelic Answer

Last March, our beautiful nineteen-month-old daughter was placed in hospice.

We knew we had a short time left with her, and our hearts were breaking.

One night she and I were asleep on the couch, and my husband was right by us on a mattress we had pulled into the living room. I woke up at three in the morning, and I remember looking at her and then getting on my knees and telling God that I needed him "to send angels to get Macy so that she wouldn't have to go alone."

I instantly felt my grandpa next to me. Then I felt my husband's grandpa up by my daughter. Her hand shot into the air and she held it there for a long time. She had never done anything like that before, and I have no doubt that she was holding his hand. I then felt a circle of angels surrounding us. My husband woke up and said he felt like he needed to come over.

Macy didn't pass that night, but I know they came to help me and my husband know that she wouldn't be alone, and to help her prepare for the other side of the veil.

BY DANIELLE MILLER

The Laws of Good Health

Only a few short months after my husband and I got married (2011), I experienced multiple major panic attacks that led to me having debilitating anxiety. My husband knew I was experiencing "anxiety" but I never truly opened up to him about it until years later.

During some of my darkest days, just trying to survive, I relied heavily on words from my patriarchal blessing that promised me good health as long as I obeyed the "laws of good health".

At the time, I thought what I was doing was following the "laws of good health", but little did I know I was far from it. I remember being in the bathroom, begging Heavenly Father to lift this burden from my shoulders for the remainder of the day so I could make it through.

Time and time again, He delivered me from my deepest, darkest despair.

One year after my first panic attack (2012), we moved to Washington State only for my husband to be deployed one month later. It was up there that I started to see

141

pieces of my prayers being answered and put together. He showed up by placing some of the most amazing people in my life; friends that you call your family.

He showed me the importance of connecting and being in nature to find healing. He made it clear how important exercise was to help me function and to feel physically and mentally better.

I was still struggling with anxiety in 2013 and it wasn't healthy. I knew it was time to take action, and I remembered the talk Elder Holland gave in 2013 General Conference: "Like a Broken Vessel", where he simply says it's okay to seek medical help if you're suffering from mental illnesses.

I knew this was God telling me it was time to go to the doctor and get on medication to help me. It took me, setting aside my pride, and a leap of faith- but I did it and I'm forever grateful. It was life changing.

Fast forward to 2018 when I was tired of carrying extra baby weight, and wanted to look better. I started working with a friend and nutrition coach who taught me more about living the "laws of good health". I started noticing that as I changed and improved what I was eating I started feeling incredibly better, mentally and physically!

By 2019, I had joined a gym where I met some friends who were talking to me about an account they followed on Instagram, where the creator talks about how she changed her diet and lifestyle- and healed her debilitating depression.

I felt like hearing these words was like angels speaking to me, telling me that what I longed for for years was right at my fingertips! I started learning, praying for guidance, and putting in the work. Soon, I found myself weaning off of my anxiety medication, and no longer taking it!

Looking back I see how I was truly guided to learn what living the "laws of good health" meant and was taken slowly, step by step, to get to the point where I now use God's creations on this earth to find healing.

I realize He was guiding me all along.

It's like that poem "Footprints in the Sand"- where there were so many times in my journey with anxiety that I felt alone or forgotten, but looking back I realize Christ was carrying me the whole way. I could have never made it to where I am today without His never-ending unconditional love. I truly have a testimony that God hears our prayers and answers them in just the right way in which we personally need. It may not be all at once, but He will never leave us alone in our journey here on this earth.

BY KELSEE BOYER

Snowflakes

When I was 15 years old, my family traveled up a canyon one weekend through dense, giant snowflakes, to go snowmobiling- as we did most weekends in winter.

This particular day, I was deep in teenage angst, battling feelings of insecurity, self-worth, and inadequacy. I have struggled with confidence in my *entire life,* but this was a stand-out time when I felt the real darkness of irrelevance in my small world of happy, motivated, up-and-coming kids.

As my family played that day, I did my best to be there, but couldn't find the joy. Each time I tried to smile, tears came instead. Then, in a brief moment toward the end of the outing, I found myself alone in the gray, at the top of a hillside bank of fresh snow.

I laid there, feeling it all, as the sounds around me faded to a quiet, peaceful stillness that I had never felt before. I stared up at the sky from my back and watched snowflakes fall, and felt them catch on my tear-streaked face.

I reached up to wipe away tears, and suddenly the

144

tiniest fleck of white caught my eye, standing out in stark contrast from my black glove.

There in the palm of my hand was the most perfect, intricately-crafted, stellar dendrite- unlike anything I'd ever seen in my life!

I brought it closer to my eyes and blinked away more tears to rid my vision of the blurry outlines. I stared in wonder at this tiny, perfect, glittering speck, that- had it not landed in my hand- would have been lost in a sea of white beneath me, never to have been beheld in its true beauty.

As I stared and marveled, the world around me grew even quieter; and suddenly a voice, so soft it couldn't have been meant for any ear to hear, whispered to my wounded heart:

"If God cares enough to put majestic beauty into this tiny snowflake, how much more do you think He cares about the creation of YOU?"

A warmth I have never again experienced spread throughout my entire body as the sun peaked out from behind the clouds, and I KNEW God was there with me.

With ME, this not-different-than-any-other-young-woman; feeling alone, at the top of a snow-covered hill, holding a snowflake.

More tears came, but this time, with a smile that hurt my cheeks.

God loved ME. God knew ME. I was His and He wanted ME to know that snowflakes matter to Him, and that I matter even more!

Present day, when I find myself in a space to reflect back on this story, that same Spirit visits me as I am quiet, and whispers, *"When you have times in life you feel you will never measure up, remember that one tiny snowflake brought God to a girl filled with trouble and heartache and reminded her of her divine worth and purpose and He'll never change His mind about her."*

And He will never change His mind about me.

BY AMBER POLLARD

He Is Already Answering Your Prayers

A while back, I didn't have any idea of my worth, and I struggled with dating. I allowed myself to be treated lower than I felt I deserved. There was one relationship that really rocked me. I felt so broken, and my hope was dwindling.

I was struggling to see the light & my testimony was suffering.

About a year after this relationship ended, I was still struggling. I remember praying to find someone again and to be treated to the level of which I was worth.

Then I met my angel husband.

I had never felt so seen.

He showed me the light I never even knew I had! Without a doubt, he changed me in so many ways. I'm so thankful to know my husband was the angel I needed to come back to church, and to know *I was never alone.* He was an answer to a prayer, and now we have been married for five years, with two beautiful girls!

147

Please know, God is watching over you.

He is already answering your prayers. Keep your eyes open to see it.

BY CANDRA WYNNE

Miracle In a Cemetery

My dad passed away suddenly and unexpectedly in January of 2021.

A few days later, my mom was trying to find a place to bury his body.

His father was buried in a cemetery near our house, but the office staff were very unpleasant to work with, and my mom didn't want to deal with their "sales tactics".

A friend of ours told us that we could look online for cemetery plots for sale by individual owners, so we did some research and found one but they could only tell us the plot number and a general area.

My mom wanted to know exactly where the plot was so we headed to the cemetery to find it. After getting nowhere with the sales office, we all felt defeated and overwhelmed.

We were slowly driving through the cemetery, deciding what to do next and I noticed a maintenance truck for the cemetery company. I had the idea to ask him if he knew where the plot was.

We pulled up next to the car and I waved at him! I put my face mask on (Covid) and walked up to the passenger side of the car, and explained our situation.

I wasn't paying attention to his face or anything else for that matter, because I was holding back my tears of frustration, and extreme sadness.

When I finished my story, *he responded by saying my name and asking if it was me.*

It was then that I looked at his face and quickly realized that it was a friend of mine from high school. I hadn't seen or spoken to him since we graduated sixteen years before.

He then said that he knew where the plot was, and to follow him. He drove us to an area, then walked us around until he found the exact plot number.

Tears streamed from our eyes as we looked around and realized that the plot was just *feet away from my grandfather's resting place.*

We talked with my friend for a few more minutes, and he told us that the location we were at wasn't his regular working location; he was just filling in for someone who was sick.

This experience reminded me that God is in every detail of our lives. That he cares about us, and even though our family didn't get to experience a miracle like Zacarius being raised from the dead- that He still per-

150

formed other miracles that would reaffirm His love for us, and our testimony in Him.

BY HALEY THEDELL

Heal, and Live Again

I had never known a pain so deep, so scary, and so real-until I faced postpartum depression after my third baby. It led to panic attacks and suicidal ideation.

I felt undeserving of all that I had, because everything I had was so beautiful; yet I didn't want to be here anymore.

This made it worse, because I thought, "There are people out there that have it so much worse than me, and they stay with no hesitation!"

I reached the point of my husband taking me to the emergency room. He gave me a priesthood blessing before we went inside. I had hit rock bottom and felt *no hope.*

Yet somehow, I began to feel hope; to come out of the fog and to rise again.

The one thought that started my healing process was that *God knew ME and loved ME.*

He understood my pain, and He didn't think any less of me because of the very real trial that I was going through.

Jesus Christ had felt every ounce of pain I felt- and got through it. So I could get through it too.

He and my Heavenly Father validated that pain, and God's hand is what reached down and helped me to get back up and to heal and live again!

BY ASHLIN PATTEN

God Meets You Where You Are

I always felt God come for me in my darkest moments in life, when the darkness was only able to be penetrated by Christ's grace and divine light!

Motherhood was always my dream- my only dream.

I couldn't wait to start a family, and when those two pink lines appeared I was elated.

The debilitating nausea and vomiting began quickly, and never left my entire pregnancy.

If only I knew then, with each baby my experience would only get worse.

By the second baby, the nausea and vomiting got worse- and I was given an IV every other day. After that sweet baby entered the world at eleven pounds, PPD peaked when he was five months old.

It was my first experience with suicidal ideation, and it was terrifying.

By baby three, I was diagnosed with Hyperemesis

Gravidarum. I had to receive a picc line and home health to manage that pregnancy.

Pregnancy number four came sooner than planned after that, and by twelve weeks, I was hospitalized for severe depression and suicidal ideation.

During these times, medication, therapy and many prayers and blessings got me through- but the depression became a part of my everyday life.

Baby number five came a couple of years later. I felt I was in a better place mentally during those months, but it was by far my hardest pregnancy. I spent weeks at a time in the hospital. I had a picc line, which ended up failing after a month; so I ended up with a feeding tube.

I had lost thirty pounds within two weeks, and most of the muscle in my legs. Many times, I had my husband carry me to the bathroom, and I spent all my time in bed.

My babies had to go live with my family in a different state during this time, because I was unable to take care of them. It was the darkest time.

But I felt God.

I saw him in the tiniest details of the pregnancy, and we saw so many miracles that I could probably write a whole book about it.

People say to me all the time: "If your pregnancies were so bad, why did you do it five times!?"

And all I can say is: "God."

Because He asked me to.

Because in the trial, He taught me.

He increased my capacity to love, have empathy and understanding.

It taught me to not only believe in Him, *but to see Him.*

Unfortunately, I wish the trials all ended with the challenges that accompanied having babies; but I'm afraid it's probably only the beginning!

Depression and anxiety are just part of who I am, and I am learning to be okay with that.

At the beginning of this year, after months of unending trials, one thing after another kept coming- and I felt lost and in that darkness once again.

This darkness felt unbeatable.

On a night a few days before my baby's first birthday, I overdosed; in hopes of ending my life. My angel husband once again saved me, and I spent a week in the hospital, recovering and stabilizing.

Today I am in a much better place. Once again, God came for me; and I know He will keep coming. *He meets you where you are no matter where you are.* You are not alone.

BY DAWN REEVE

On the Aisles of Costco

2020 was not hard because of "the virus"- but because of a virus that was infecting my family: pornography addiction.

After years of therapy, a twelve-step program and counseling, my marriage finally ended. I was forced to find a new home in thirty days, when the world is on lockdown, uprooting my children, their schools, my neighbors, friends and support system.

Our new home was a brand new beautiful basement with walkout doors.

So I accepted sleeping on the floor in the storage closet. *He was there.*

Only three months later, we were notified that the landlord couldn't have two renters and we had moved again; but this time, to a dark basement with too many spiders and centipedes to count.

During the same month, my dad passed away unexpectedly- allowing me to feel the deepest pain and sorrow I have felt thus far in my life. It was getting too hard to bear.

I needed to put on my "game face" and be brave for

my three children, but it was a struggle to wake up or to even *want* to wake up.

I knew my Savior was there but I felt so alone.

Christmas came around, and I was in a new ward, trying to make new memories for my kids. However, with the little money I had, I knew it would look different than in previous years.

One day, we were walking around Costco (because that's what you do when you have kids and it's cold outside) and I saw this beautiful all-white picture of Jesus, standing out in the water. I fell in love with it. It was one of many incredible pictures, but when I saw this one I said: "When I get money, that will be in my house someday."

As the month passed, we were showered with *two* "Twelve Days of Christmas" gifts and surprises by so many neighbors. We felt so seen and loved by these people we didn't know. On the last day of Christmas, December the 24th, there was one gift, wrapped on my porch.

The kids and I had received so much, we wondered what this last gift could possibly be. What could this kind neighbor (who knows nothing about me) pick out for me?

And there it was. The white picture of Jesus on the water.

The picture from Costco I hoped in my heart I would have one day.

Only God knew that. He made it perfectly clear. *He knows me.* Not just who I am, but He knows my heart. Personally and intimately. He knows me. I just started bawling.

Even when life is hard and dark and you can't see the light at the end of the tunnel, He is there- walking down the aisles of Costco, listening to your heart.

He was there. He has always been there, and He will walk with you *every single step of this life journey.* He came for this single mother of three, living in a dark basement on Christmas Eve. He met me where I was at. *And He will come for you too.* Exactly where you are.

BY HEATHER DONEY

Encircled in the Arms of His Love

When I was twenty-one years old, I was really struggling with my testimony in the Church of Jesus Christ of Latter-day Saints. I didn't know what I believed anymore. I was waiting for my boyfriend who was serving a mission, but I didn't feel worthy of him. I hadn't been making the best choices. I was so confused.

One night I spent a very long time praying. Like praying and crying with all my might for an answer. I wanted to know if the church was true. I had been raised in the church, but living out on my own for a couple of years really put me to the test on what I believed.

I told God I needed to know, and I needed help to feel my worth, and the Spirit again. The song "Where Can I Turn For Peace" came to my mind. I opened up the back of my scriptures and looked up the word "Peace" in the topical guide.

A scripture stuck out to me so I turned to it. It was in Section 6 of the Doctrine and Covenants. I decided to read the whole Section instead of just that verse. I have never in my life read something in the scriptures that I felt pertained to me at that very moment, until that night.

The Lord was speaking right to me!

Verse 20: *"I have spoken unto thee because of thy desires; therefore treasure up these words in thy heart. Be faithful and diligent in keeping the commandments of God, and I will encircle thee in the arms of my love.*

Verse 21: *"Behold, I am Jesus Christ, the Son of God. I am the same that came unto mine own, and mine own received me not. I am the light which shineth in darkness, and the darkness comprehendeth it not."*

Verse 22: *"Verily, verily, I say unto you, if you desire a further witness, cast your mind upon the night that you cried unto me in your heart, that you might know concerning the truth of these things."*

Verse 23: *"Did I not speak peace to your mind concerning the matter? What greater witness can you have than from God?"*

Anytime, I get doubts, I immediately think of verses 22 and 23!

I will never forget that He came to me and answered my prayers and made me feel worthy to receive an answer, even when I felt so unworthy.

I literally felt like He encircled me in the arms of His love.

I'm so grateful for a loving God and Son who will come to us in our lowest of lows and lift us up. (And PS. I later married that sweet missionary I was waiting for, and we've been married for 23 years.)

BY ELIZABETH OLSON

Carried, Held and Guided

One night during my postpartum journey with my second child, while laying in bed, I had a spontaneous panic attack.

At the time I had no idea what a panic attack was, or what it was like to experience one. All I knew was that I felt like I had fallen into a black abyss, and I had never felt so alone in my entire life- despite laying next to my sleeping husband.

At that moment, the only thing I could think of was to pray.

I said "God, I need to know that you're there."

And like a flash of light, suddenly the air was clear and I felt the most calm, peaceful feeling wash over me. Then I said "God, I need to be able to breathe."

And I was able to take a giant refreshing breath.

I then prayed, "God, I need to sleep."

And I was able to roll over, close my eyes and fall into a deep sleep.

A few days later, I was reminiscing on the experience and a thought came to my head:

"You are going through this so you can teach others."

Although I feel unqualified and unsure that I'm saying the right things, I've felt reassured because of the enabling power of the atonement. I've been carried, held and guided.

BY NIKKI JEMMETT

He Cried With Me

In November of 2020, we found out we were going to have triplets!

We were shocked- to say the least- triplets without fertility medication is not super common! We were scared to death, but so excited and blessed.

I was able to see their heartbeats in an ultrasound: the most beautiful thing I've ever seen!

Around 10 weeks I went into a high-risk doctor appointment. It was still during covid, so my husband could not come in with me.

As soon as I entered the room, I knew something was wrong. I laid on the table to get ready for the ultrasound. I first saw the "singleton" baby, looking like a gummy bear, wiggling all over. Then she moved to the twins, and immediately I knew they were gone.

They were smaller and not moving like I had seen just a week prior. It is hard to put into words what I felt at that moment. This is when I first felt the Lord's hand. He comforted me enough to make it through the rest of the ultrasound without losing it.

I was able to make it to the car where my husband was. As soon as I opened the door I just kept saying through the tears, "My babies!" This would be the second time I felt the Lord's hand.

In this excruciatingly painful moment, my husband and I felt comfort, love and peace amongst the pain and sadness. The months following were filled with many moments like this.

As I look back, I clearly see the Lord's hand being present through this hardship that we are still going through. Many times, I felt distanced from the Lord, and then so very connected and close.

I felt Him right next to me, *knowing he cried with me,* comforted me, and loved me through.

BY DEANNA CLUFF

He Is Always Aware

In the darkest of times, He is always there.

So many nights I've spent in the hospital with my oldest son. He prayed with me, and his prayers were always answered. When all felt lost and I couldn't handle anymore, I asked Jesus to take it for me. And he did. A weight was lifted almost immediately.

I can't even explain it. Our situation hadn't changed, my son wasn't healed immediately, *but the heaviness lifted.* I could keep going and be there for my son. I could be his advocate and just love him as much as possible.

During those times, people prayed and fasted for my son and our family. We were lifted in prayer. We felt the love of our Savior, and I know He is always aware of us.

We just need to turn to Him.

I miss how close I felt to my Savior; but I know He is always there!

BY MISSY ALLRED

A Broken Vessel

I've struggled with my mental health, pretty much as long as I can remember.

I have a memory from about fifth grade, where I clearly remember thinking, "Something is wrong with me. My head should not be like this."

From there it got worse. I went on antidepressants as a young teenager to help keep my mind at bay. By my junior year in high school I was absolutely drowning. Everything looked perfect on the outside: perfect grades, extracurriculars, a loving boyfriend (who later became my husband), and supportive family; but inside I was done.

One night, I got up to make it all stop.

Right as I was getting out of bed, an image of my boyfriend, and then my mom, flashed across my mind - and I knew I couldn't do that to them. I got right back into bed and cried myself to sleep. That was miracle number one.

Within a couple of weeks, it was General Conference. My family was a few minutes behind, and my phone started blowing up from texts from my boyfriend making sure I was listening to Elder Holland's talk.

The talk that year was "Like a Broken Vessel" and it felt like it was meant just for me.

My mom and I sobbed through the whole thing as she held me. It was the answer to both of our prayers for years. That talk was a turning point for me- not just in my mental health, but in my relationship with the Savior. *I have never again doubted if He was there or if He was aware of me.*

Stay

When I was six months pregnant with my youngest, I came home from work and found my husband at home sitting on the couch. He was never home before me. He said, "We need to talk."

He took me into our room, and told me he had been having an affair with my friend for the last three years, and that he had a pornography addiction.

I was blindsided.

I've never seen so much pain in someone's eyes than at that moment.

I didn't know what to do, or if I should stay or leave. I went to my closet and knelt down to pray. I told my Heavenly Father that I wasn't in a good place and that I knew I couldn't make a decision on how I felt at that moment.

I asked what He wanted me to do. Clear as day I heard Him say, *"Stay."*

And throughout the next few years as I fought for my marriage, the Savior came to me.

He came to me in the form of a visiting teacher, dropping by with my favorite treat and a friend, bringing a gift titled "Surrounded by Love" because she felt the Spirit tell her to.

He held me as I cried in my room. He never left me alone in my darkest moments. Looking back, *I see even more of Him in the details.*

BY MADELINE CASEY

The Parent in the Other Room

My husband had the once-in-a-lifetime opportunity to hike Mt Kilimanjaro with his brothers. At first, I was very against it. I didn't want him to go, because it's so far away, and it would be for two and a half weeks.

As a mom of two kids, I knew how much work that would be; but, I realized that if I was in his position, I would want him to encourage me to go and to have the adventure of a lifetime- so I told him to go!

The biggest worry for me was dinner and bedtime. Every person who cares for children knows that this can be the hardest time of day! My husband and I usually each take one kid and we switch off every night. Some nights, our youngest can take over an hour to get to bed.

I knew the kids and I would be exhausted, so I tried to come up with a plan beforehand to make sure it went smoothly. I prayed every day for help with

171

patience and love for my sweet kids, as we navigated this tricky time of night.

Every time I put them to bed, *it went incredibly smooth.*

Every night that my husband was gone was the easiest bedtime routine I had ever done!

I started to think, "Wow, this isn't so hard! I can put them to bed by myself!

And then I thought, *"I haven't been doing it by myself, God has been the parent in the other room."*

It was a sweet reminder that He cares for me and my family, that He is happy to help- even with the littlest things. All I have to do is ask.

BY RACHEL KUNZ

He Came With Me

As grief felt unbearable, He came for me through a sunset that connected me to the ones I love on the other side of the veil.

Little and uncertain about why other children didn't want to be my friend on the playground, He sat with me as I watched others laugh and play.

Walking individually down the halls, and showing honesty in test-taking, He told me to believe it was for a greater reason that I didn't 'fit in'.

The nights when even the stars felt dim and scarce, He came and shined His heavenly light for me to feel.

Looking back, He didn't come for me, He came WITH me.

BY AUBREE BOSEN

God Unites Families

After a bumpy road, I had the privilege of becoming pregnant.

I was convinced it was twins. I was having consistent dreams of a little girl with brown hair, and a little boy with black hair, holding hands and playing with each other.

Coincidently, the same week my mom and brother told me that they were having similar dreams about me having boy and girl twins.

So, when I went in for my twenty week ultrasound, I was convinced the ultrasound tech didn't know what she was doing when she insisted that I just had ONE little girl, floating around in there.

I was confident she missed something. My dreams were so real.

I had the strongest feeling that two babies were coming.

So I did what any irrational person would do:

I bought two of everything.

Two carseats, two cribs, a double stroller.

Everyone thought I was crazy. I even thought I was crazy, but I KNEW the spirit was telling me to be prepared.

A few weeks after my ultrasound, we had a friend approach us and ask if we would be willing to adopt her baby! I thought, "This must be what we were preparing for!"

My husband and I didn't even think twice when we said, "YES!" in unison.

We immediately jumped into gear and got our home study and background checks completed. However, as time went on, she realized we weren't the right choice for her baby, and I felt the same.

However, she is the angel that prepared us for what was to come.

By this point, my beautiful daughter was born. I had no answers as to where the little boy was, but we had so much occupying our minds, I pushed those thoughts away.

My husband and I decided to go to the temple and see if we could receive any guidance on what to do. I prayed so hard that I could get some sort of clarity.

I was doing everything I felt God was asking of me, but it felt like I was running full-speed with a blindfold on, and I was tired.

As I sat in the temple, I looked up to see a painting that featured Jesus holding onto a little girl with brown hair, and a little boy with black hair.

I knew that God wasn't done with me. I had to keep running forward at full-speed.

My husband and I walked out of that session, and both looked at each other and said,

"He's coming!"

Not even a week later, I was sitting in church when an unknown number started calling me. Against my typical self, I walked out of Sunday School to answer.

It was a lawyer.

"Hi, I saw a profile on your family. I am with a woman right now who is in labor. She is dilated to a seven. She is wanting you to adopt her baby. Are you still hoping to adopt?"

I didn't know anything about this woman or child and I didn't know if it was a boy. I didn't know his hair color; *but, I had the warmest feeling come over me.*

That night, I flew across the country with a three-month-old, to meet my black-haired son. He looked just like my dream.

Eight years later, and many more miracles and Godly interventions, we still have an open adoption AND we are now raising three more of my son's siblings.

We didn't just adopt a son, we became a family- with his birth mother and all.

God truly does unite families.

BY ANONYMOUS

He Will Pull Us Through the Dark

My father started drinking when I was eight-years-old. He was a great father, but when he was drunk, it was scary. I was often scared as a kid, alone, and many nights would cry myself to sleep.

Life had good times, but we still had very hard days.

I would pray that my dad would stop drinking and hanging out with the people he made those choices with. I loved him but his choices hurt our family

Fast forward to when I was fourteen. I went to EFY, and the first night there, our counselor challenged us to pray for an answer to a question we had.

My question was: *"Is God really there, and does he really love and care about me"?*

Everyday, while at EFY, I prayed a lot and wasn't feeling an answer until the last devotional night. My best friend that went with me was saying the closing prayer.

I remember in that prayer, all I heard was: "Heavenly Father loves you, Heavenly Father knows what you are going through, He cares about you, He wants you to rely on him."

Over and over I heard he loved me and I started bawling.

Afterwards, I went to my friend and gave her a big hug and said I needed to hear that. I knew that the Lord used my friend to answer my prayer.

Now as an adult, I hold this experience dear to me, and know that He is there if we will turn to him. Now as my dad is struggling with a new addiction, I have had to set boundaries.

It's hard, and I pray for him always. I have to re-mind myself of that 14 year old girl who was told "The Lord knows me and cares for me!"

He will help us and come to us when we are in need, but we need to act in Faith. Sometimes, the only choice is to just keep trusting and keep going! He will help pull us through the dark.

BY MADDISON DYE

Healing Through Creating

Postpartum OCD, anxiety and depression is a dark place.

I was in this darkness after the birth of each of my 4 children, but after my first baby was born I didn't know what was going on in my brain.

I didn't understand why I felt the way I did. On top of that, I was a full-time college student. My husband was also a full-time college student and working part-time.

It was also winter in Northern Utah, so I wasn't able to get out of the house often.

My son nursed for forty minutes, every two hours-day and night, so I was exhausted.

My day consisted of nursing and trying to cram everything into those two hours between each feeding. After feeding my baby I could do homework, clean the house, take care of other business, shower, eat, or sleep.

Homework had a deadline, so it always won- and cleaning the house came next.

I was hardly sleeping and I definitely wasn't eating enough. At one point I only weighed ninety six pounds. I pleaded with Heavenly Father for help. I had no idea I was struggling with mental health, but I knew something was wrong.

One day as I finished nursing my baby and put him down for a nap, I started cleaning up my house.

I was so exhausted that I felt like I was seeing people in my house. I knew I needed to sleep, so I laid down and started drifting off to sleep.

Before I fell asleep I got this vivid mental image in my mind of a boy in the middle of some sand dunes. I got up and pulled out my computer. I had to know this boy's story, and the only way I could know was by creating it.

That was the start of my first fantasy novel!

That experience taught me the power of creating when it comes to managing my mental health.

When I write my fantasy books, I am able to get out of my own head and into the mind of my characters. It stops my OCD cycles and pulls me out of depression, even if it's only for the time that I'm writing.

Heavenly Father didn't take away my mental illness; in fact it got so much worse before it got better, but He reached down and showed me *a tool I can use when I start to spiral.*

I'm sure that image in my head was Him- guiding me to *find a bit of relief through creating.*

I know He is with us in our struggles. He is anxious

to help us even if it's not in the way we expect. I wanted Him to take away my pain, but in a way, He provided me with something much better.

He gave me a testimony that He is with me and wants to help me. He gave me a tool to use when I'm struggling, and He gave me a hobby that I love.

BY CARRIE WILLIAMS

He Came For Me Through Others

2022 was the hardest year of my life, but also the year that I felt Christ the most.

Toward the end of 2021, my husband, Kenny, started to have pain in his hip and back.

He is a police officer so he figured the weight of his gear was starting to affect him. He tried going to the chiropractor, but the pain just kept getting worse.

He was sent to his primary care doctor who eventually ordered an MRI, to try to see what was going on. His MRI was on January 19th.

That was the day our lives changed forever.

I was able to see the results of the MRI before any doctor did. I am a nurse, but really had no idea what the MRI was saying, besides it being abnormal.

I asked a few doctor friends if they knew, but it

was hard to tell what it meant. I felt prompted to text a spine doctor who my husband was getting referred to. He immediately looked at the MRI and called me. Even though Kenny wasn't even his patient yet, he cared enough to call the primary doctor, and told him to order multiple tests and labs.

He got us in sooner than our original appointment- still scheduled for a few weeks away. He was in so much pain that when he got home from work, he could barely walk.

I remember one day the pain was so bad that I called my dad to give him a blessing.

My boss lives close and I knew he was home, so I asked him to help my dad. Kenny was finally able to sleep that day, and even though his pain was still there, he had some relief.

It took almost two months to get a diagnosis for my husband.

I remember sitting in a Sacrament meeting during a fast and testimony meeting on March 6th. I felt the Spirit so strong, and I was just sitting there crying during other people's testimonies. I looked down at my watch to see that the spine doctor had texted me.

He told me the pathologist was in his ward and had told him the pathology reports from the last test. He wanted to FaceTime after church.

He diagnosed my husband with leukemia, and said he couldn't really answer any questions because he wasn't an oncologist.

He bore us his testimony on how families are together

forever and how we can do hard things. I know most doctors don't relate the gospel as they are giving a cancer diagnosis, but it did help put things into perspective.

Two days later, we were sent two hours away to Huntsman Cancer Center to begin treatment. We left our four-year-old daughter and ten-month-old son. We had never spent a night away from our baby. I didn't know how I was going to do this. I went two weeks without seeing my kids.

Christ came to me as my mom dropped everything to watch my kids.

Her coworkers picked up her shifts so that she could watch my kids.

Kenny's co-workers organized a huge fundraiser to help make up for lost pay.

My coworkers covered my shifts.

Kenny spent most of March, April and May in and out of the hospital. No chemo was working. The pain was getting worse, and it was so discouraging. It seemed like nothing the doctors were trying was working! He needed a bone marrow transplant, but needed to have most of the cancer gone first.

I made so many trips back and forth to Utah. People asked me how I was so strong. I usually felt numb when people would talk to me. I would break down after I left my husband alone in the hospital to go back to my kids and my job. I would listen to church music and just cry.

Those are the moments I felt Christ helping me the most.

He taught me through music, that I was not alone and that I could do hard things.

184

After months of prepping for a bone marrow transplant, Kenny was able to get the transplant on November 17th. He had to stay down in Utah for three months after the transplant.

I remember trying to pack up my two kids and a dog to go spend ten days in Utah for Christmas and New Year's. I was feeling so overwhelmed. I was so over being a single mom, and feeling guilty for leaving Kenny alone.

I heard a knock on my door and saw a present. I opened it up and read the note and started to cry. We were supposed to go to Disneyland in October, but didn't make it because of cancer. There was a Mickey Mouse cup, Disney stickers, a hot chocolate bomb, and lots of candy.

The note said: "I know you didn't make it to Disneyland this year, but I hope this gift may give you some Disney magic for the holidays."

I just sat there and lost it. My friend must have known how hard of a day I was having.

A couple of weeks later after the holidays, I finally made time to have the hot cocoa.

I opened it up and cried again. She had special ordered a Minnie Mouse-themed bomb. It just meant so much that she had gone out of her way to make it special for me.

There were so many days where Christ came for me.

Whether it was someone bringing us dinner, sending us money, watching our kids, paying for my shampoo, or even just buying me a soda pop.

My husband was able to come home a couple of weeks ago, and he is now cancer-free.

We couldn't have made it through the last year without Christ being there for us- usually through other peoples' service.

BY SHERELYN CURETON

These Are My Children, All will Be Well

Several years ago I was raising my two grandchildren, and was struggling with their Mother over her addictions. It was a low point, because I realized she did not want her children back at all.

They came to me so abused.

I felt like I was sinking in the process of change. They were five and six years old when the State came to me and said, "Take them today, or they go to the state."

I was angry with my daughter for what happened. I cried, prayed, and petitioned the Lord for healing. This happened over a period of time.

Over the course of a year, I became distraught, but through many prayers I received the answer.

As I slept one particular night, a vision was opened to me in a dream.

I was walking with the Savior. It was comforting and filled with a love I have never known. He told me, *"These are my children, all will be well."*

His love enveloped me.

BY ANGELINA BRIGGS

He Already Came

I remember feeling really angry, forgotten and alone.

I felt like I was being punished for something I didn't do, and I couldn't understand why. Heavenly Father left me when I felt like I needed him most and I remember the guilt that followed.

How could I be feeling this way when I've been so blessed?

I had a healthy baby, loving husband, warm home, flexible job, family support, and the list goes on and on. Yet, somehow, life was still dark.

I remember prayer after prayer; I just felt more and more empty and alone.

Then one day as I was praying, crying for help and desperately asking, "Where are you?!"

I remember seeing in my mind a picture of Christ in Gethsemane.

Then I had the thought, *"He already came. He's already here."*

It was then I realized that He already did it!

I didn't need to question where He was or the help I was so desperate for, because it was already here. I didn't need to see the Heaven's open and pour down blessings, because they already had.

Heavenly help, comfort and guidance were already mine; that was settled in Gethsemane long ago.

I realized then, that Christ doesn't come and go depending on when we need Him.

He may quietly be listening or comforting, but never abandoning.

He did, and is doing, His job- and now it's our job to trust Him.

It's our job to use the enabling power of the Atonement to not only take away pain and suffering, but to make us strong enough to overcome it.

To come to Him.

I'm so grateful for a loving Heavenly Father who is patient with me. I'm grateful for a Savior who came for me long before I came to Him, and I'm grateful that He stays.

BY JAYMIE MAINES

Not Alone

I entered the new role of motherhood in a very unique way. My first-born baby boy came and left this earth in complete heartbreaking silence.

Born at six pounds, six ounces with a perfect body, I was unable to mother him in the ways that I had planned.

I remember the days leading up to his funeral were filled with anger and despair. I closed the newly finished nursery door, and tried to make plans and necessary arrangements for the coming days.

I remember standing in the shower with a broken postpartum body, crying as my milk came in. I felt so broken. I was unable to breathe. I had never experienced such deep pain.

I spoke to my mom as I was being buried by my grief. She told me to let Heavenly Father carry the pain. She told me to tell Heavenly Father how angry I was. I remember her saying that Heavenly Father can take it. He can take the anger and sadness.

I went and knelt by my bed, and really had it out with God.

I told him how unbearable this was.

I told him how angry I was with him.

As my heart screamed, I remember feeling the distinct feeling that He understood. *Christ felt my despair.* He understood and wanted to carry it for me.

For the first time in my life, I felt like He really knew me as an individual. Christ experienced mortality to truly understand the pain and heartache we would feel.

I was not doing this alone.

Subsequently, three more babies have joined our family. I believe my first experience has caused me to worry excessively, but has given me the opportunity to more fully rely on Him.

It has also helped me to truly understand the love our Heavenly Father has for me and my children. Though nothing has been as difficult as those days, I have often knelt down and really let my Heavenly Father know how I am feeling, and have pleaded for his guidance, love and protection as I do my best to raise my other children.

I know I am not doing this alone. I know He knows our heartache and struggle, and will help us.

When our hearts are tired, I know He is there to carry them. Not only will he carry us, but one day, He will make all things right.

Motherhood changed me. Christ changed me. Christ still changes me, as I know He carries me through one of the most sacred callings given to women; to be a mother.

BY EMILY JOY BELL
{1986- 2023}

Be Still and Know

One particular day, a few weeks after my cancer diagnosis, I could feel my heart desperately crying for peace.

I needed a respite, a reset, a quick retreat. I don't remember where Colby (my husband) and the kids were, but I asked my dad if I could borrow his car, and I escaped to the temple- a familiar, sacred place of worship.

After many prayers I settled into myself. My mind was on rapid-fire, petitioning God with a cacophony of questions:

"What should I do? Am I going to die? How long am I going to live? What will my family do? Will my kids remember their mom? Will I see them graduate high school? Get married? Will I know my grandchildren? What about Colby? Why did this happen? What do you want me to learn?"

There was sheer frenzied panic inside, and all of a sudden, these words cut through my noisy mind like a knife through cheesecake; silent, soft and easy, and yet firm at the same time.

"Be still and know that I am God."

"But what…" I blubbered, desperate to have my questions answered.

Before I could finish, the words repeated firmly, *"Be still and know that I am God."*

The words came again. And again. And again. *"Be still and know that I am God. Be still and know that I am God. Be still and know that I am God."*

As long as I resumed my frantic queries, the words repeated.

Finally, I realized they weren't stopping, and my protests were futile. The words seemed to come from within me and somehow somewhere outside of me, much higher than me at the same time, firmly, and yet gently shushing my panic and distilling peace through my soul like the effects of a sedative, slowly spreading through me.

I surrendered, and let myself bask in the hypnotizing repeat of the words. I noticed they seemed to have a rhythm to them; like the waves of the ocean, they rolled in gently, and rolled out, and came back in the same way, in and out.

"Be still and know that I am God. Be still and know that I am God. Be still and know that I am God. Be STILL and KNOW that I am God."

I breathed a deep sigh of relief and calm, the questions no longer throbbing in my brain.

Where they had just been, there was a warm, white, radiant peace. I felt totally relaxed.

I looked around then, and I saw people all around me - people I hadn't noticed before.

Suddenly I saw them differently, like I had removed some lenses that had been obstructing my view.

One man looked hunched over, like the Hunchback of Notre Dame, and my heart swelled with love- and I felt full and aware of infinite potential within me and within him- and all around me, connecting us all.

I saw one couple holding hands and instantly felt their sorrow, sadness and pain.

The inner chaos I had just known was gone, and in its place there was just quiet love, light and peace.

I returned to the car with a new buoyancy in my soul. I almost felt like I was floating, but I felt intimately myself. The leaves seemed brighter, the sky bluer, the clouds more fluffy and the air cleaner and new.

In a happy trance I went through the motions, un-locking, climbing in and starting the car, ignorant to the radio my dad had left playing.

I must have driven twenty minutes to the temple with it playing before, so lost in the incessant noise of my thoughts, that I didn't realize it was on.

I never listened to the radio.

Normally I would have turned it off instantly, irritat-ed by the constant interruption of commercials and chat-ter. Normally I had too much noise in my own mind to add any more. Suddenly I noticed the first song to play upon my return to the car.

The familiar words, sung by Mariah Carey and Whitney Houston, caught my attention;

Many nights we prayed
With no proof, anyone could hear
In our hearts a hopeful song
We barely understood
Now, we are not afraid
Although we know there's much to fear
We were moving mountains
Long before we knew we could, whoa, yes

There can be miracles
When you believe
Though hope is frail, it's hard to kill
Who knows what miracles you can achieve?
When you believe, somehow you will
You will when you believe

In this time of fear
When prayer so often proves in vain
Hope seems like the summer bird
Too swiftly flown away
Yet now I'm standing here
My hearts so full, I can't explain
Seeking faith and speaking' words
I never thought I'd say

There can be miracles
When you believe (When you believe)
Though hope is frail, it's hard to kill
Who knows what miracles you can achieve? (You can achieve)
When you believe, somehow you will
You will when you believe

They don't always happen when you ask
And it's easy to give in to your fears
But when you're blinded by your pain
Can't see the way, get through the rain
A small but still, resilient voice
Says, help is very near, oh

There can be miracles
When you believe
Though hope is frail
It's hard to kill
Who knows what miracles
You can achieve
When you believe somehow you will
Now, you will
You will when you
Believe
Just believe
You will when you
Believe

I cried the whole drive home, grateful for the peace.

Emily's Vision

Emily became a dear friend of mine and during the publishing process of the book, she left this life at thirty-six years old, leaving behind her husband and three kids.

She taught me so much in the short amount of time that I knew her. And although I might have shown up to help her clean her house, rub her feet, or laugh and cry at her bedside any chance I could - she was the one who saved me.

Despite the heart-wrenching suffering she endured, she never lost her faith.

She believed to her core that she was going to live.

What a beautiful way to die knowing that you're going to live.

And she does. He came for her.

She shared this vision during some of her most painful suffering that she was willing to let me share:

"I sit on the floor of a dark cave
alone and afraid, withering away.

198

My soul felt cracked, bruised and broken beyond repair.
And I was alone there.
My soul was full of despair.
The rocks beneath me sit, jagged and sharp they pierced me.
I had not even the strength to muster a shiver in the cold.
Then I lifted my chin, and my eyes caught sight
      Of a light.
It seemed I had been sitting alone for so long,
I barely dared indulge in the hopeful song;
But as the light drew near,
      I saw Him there.
He was aglow. The white light engulfed Him with an exquisite glow,
      as He stood before me.
I mumbled apologetic words of defeat.
"I'm sorry."
"I couldn't do it."
"I wasn't strong enough," came my disparaging cries.
"I'm sorry."
"Please forgive me."
      He put a finger to my lips. He didn't say a word.
But I knew my apologies and explanations weren't needed.
I didn't have the strength to stand.
But with my eyes, I looked at Him and pleaded.
He knew my request, and he scooped my frail body
      into His arms-
wrapping me in His light, His glow, leading the way back to the
blazing light of day,
when I felt the warm sun on my face.
Well- wrapped in His embrace, tears of gratitude stream down
my cheeks.

My strength was somehow miraculously renewed.
        And He sat me down gently.
As I gleefully took in the view, my soul began to doubt.
*My body began to dance and sway, and I began to shimmer in the
light of day.*
        He smiled at me, so happy to see me sort of free.
And I fell to his feet and I wept,
"Thank you."
"Thank you for rescuing me."
When my joy was full, and my tears all cried,
We laid under a tree, side by side.
        And I slept. Grateful to be alive.

A Personal Invitation

As you read these accounts of the Savior coming to these women, I hope you are able to relate it to your own life, as you ponder the times you have felt Him.

I hope it encourages you to be an instrument in His hands and gives you hope to continue looking for evidence of Him in your life every day, even in seemingly small ways.

I pray you will come to know Him and how often He comes to you.

Please use these pages to write down your experiences, big and small; to document your own story of Christ coming to you.

In your closet, bathroom, long drives, or kitchen floors. I pray you feel Him.

How Christ Has Come For Me

"I love the three words, "She turned herself." And all of us sooner or later, turn ourselves from the empty tomb, which represent... For us, a lot of times, that means a good thing, it's empty. But in my life, in your life, we have our empty tombs, things we look into and there's nothing there, but darkness, the empty tomb. She turned from it to the living Christ. And in that one brief moment of time, you have the great turning from sorrow to joy, from despair to peace. Celebratory joy, unexpected joy. The apostles, when they first see Jesus believed not for joy. So great. On the cross, Jesus said, "It is finished." And all of us, because he said it, we'll all be able to say of our own pain, whatever it is, it is finished."
S. Michael Wilcox

Acknowledgements

Publishing this book has been such an incredible experience. I see myself as just a regular mom who is willing to do what the Lord asks. When He asked me to do this book, I knew I couldn't do it alone. After years of writing in the margins of motherhood and running a business, my friend Lori Adams sent me the artwork for the cover on Christmas Eve of last year. It was the push I needed to finish this project.

A huge thank you to Maren Droubay for editing the book, and Jenessa Kramer for the graphic design.

To the many moms who submitted to this book, and those who are published in this book, thank you for sharing your experiences, and being vulnerable in order to breed connection and offer hope to women and mothers everywhere- that Christ still comes. You are the reason why this book exists, and I'm so grateful for your willingness to share your story and testimony with the world.

A huge thank you to my incredible husband and babies who have taught me more than I could ever imagine; and to my wonderful extended family who has always believed in me, and supported all of my wild ideas. To my Father-in-Law, Carl Grossen, for being my scripture library, and my dad, Kevin Olsen, for doing the legal work and believing in anything I ever do.

And to you, the reader of this book. Thank you for your incredible support. I'm honored, knowing that this book is in your hands.

-Aubrey

About The Author

AUBREY GROSSEN is a seeker of light, founder of ANYA, author of multiple published works, and inspirational speaker. She's a wife and mama to 4 littles and 2 angel babies. After going through severe postpartum depression and anxiety she knew there was something she needed to do to help others who felt the same. Since then she has been able to create a community of tens of thousands of women/moms and offer the tools to help with their mental health and find faith and hope in Jesus Christ. You can find her mostly on Instagram @aubreygrossen where she connects with other women as she shares about her motherhood and faith.

Made in United States
Troutdale, OR
10/25/2023